The Southern California
Month-by-Month
Flower Gardening Book

by Margaret Redfield

J. P. Tarcher, Inc.
Los Angeles, California

To My Mother,
Ida Hutchinson Pace

"God gave his children memory
That in life's garden there might be
June roses in December."

Acknowledgments: Portions of the sections
on composting, watering, and ground
covers have appeared in the *Los Angeles
Times Home Magazine* under the following
titles: "A Sense of Humus," "The Art of
Watering," "Easier Ways to Water," and
"Keep 'em Covered." "The Art of Watering"
has been reprinted in *Paragraphs and
Themes* by P. Joseph Canavan, D.C. Heath
and Company, 1975, Lexington, Mass.

Design and illustrations by The Committee
Typesetting by Omega Repro

Printing and binding by
Griffin Printing and Lithograph Co., Inc.

Library of Congress Catalog Card Number: 75-5301
ISBN: 0-87477-040-8

Manufactured in the United States of America

Published by J.P. Tarcher, Inc.
9110 Sunset Boulevard
Los Angeles, California 90069

1 2 3 4 5 6 7 8 9 0

The Gardening Arts

Starting from Seeds and Bedding Plants 8
Weeding 16
Mulching 18
Fertilizing and Soil Improvement 27
Propagation from Softwood Cuttings 30
Pest Control 32
Eat Your Plant and Have It Too: Pickled Nasturtium Seeds 34
Staking 39
Pinching Back 41
Eat Your Plant and Have It Too: Geranium Tea 44
Eat Your Plant and Have It Too: Sunflower Seeds 46
Watering 52
Light Up the Night with a Garden of White 54
Eat Your Plant and Have It Too: Daylilies 56
Cutting Roses for Bouquets 61
Easier Ways to Water 62
Semi-hardwood Cuttings 73
Caring for Sprinklers and Nozzles 75
Eat Your Plant and Have It Too: Violet Tea 85
Growing Ground Covers 86
Composting 94
Growing Wild Flowers 96
Selecting Tulips 104
Using Edging Plants 106
Bulb Covers 114
Tool Care 123
Glossary 131
Index 133

January

February

March

April

May

June

July

August

September

October

November

December

The Year Is a Clock

Most introductions start with, How do you do? This one starts with, How do you do it? And why?

How do you garden in Southern California to get the best results for the least work, and have the most fun while you're about it?

Why is Southern California gardening so special that it takes up a whole book?

First, some words for the Why's:

Why a Southern California gardening book? Why not write a book for the whole state? Because Southern California's climate is unique. Here year-round gardening is not only possible but downright irresistible. This is a climate of such abundant, continuous productivity that even nongardeners moving into this area find themselves reaching as enthusiastically for seeds and bulbs and bedding plants as they do for golf clubs or tennis rackets.

This book is designed to help everyone with that urge to plant. No experience necessary! All we ask is that you toss out all those "green thumb" theories and get down to the root of the matter. Plants *want* to grow for you. The color of your thumb hasn't a thing to do with it. It's the soil and the water and the amount of sun or shade that make the difference between a plant that's not really flexing its muscles, and the other kind that's full of the old get-up-and-grow!

People keep moving to Southern California—can you blame them? Many come from states where rigorous winters limit gardening to a few brief months. Even those who come here from the northern or central parts of California have been accustomed to a planting climate that differs substantially from this one.

What, exactly, do we mean when we refer to *the Southern California area?* Charles Lee, Botanical Information Consultant for the Los Angeles State and County Arboretum, defines it this way:

"Roughly, it's the area from as far north as Santa Barbara, straight across the Santa Monica mountains to the San Gabriel mountains, right on out to the San Bernardino area; from the valley south of the Santa Monica mountains to the coast, continuing to the Mexican border.

"The environment from Glendale south will be pretty much the same as from San Bernardino to Santa Barbara—no snowfall, no late frosts (the last frost usually about the middle of March). There will be variations, of course; some areas might have frost later than mid-March, or even snowfall. But basically it is an area where the same types of gardening conditions exist."

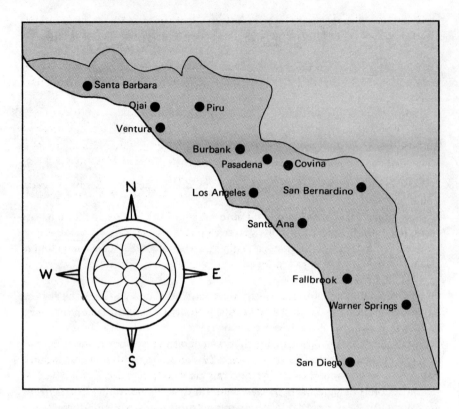

High desert and low desert are not covered in the book, because gardening in those areas is rather specialized.

The warm and wonderful world of gardening demands only a love of the good earth, a desire for creativity, and a knowledge of the three basics: food, water, and a tender discipline. Some plants want rather rich "food" (growing conditions), while others will root around happily in almost any old soil. Really! Ask any nasturtium! Proper watering is just a matter of knowing which plants are the thirsty types and which ones like things a bit on the dry side. As for discipline, it's just as important for plants as for people. Every time you stake a chrysanthemum, pinch back a seedling, divide a clump of iris, or prune a rose bush, you're exercising the sort of discipline or control that keeps the garden at its best.

And it's all a lot easier than it sounds. Come along with me; we'll skip some of those garden jobs you always thought *had* to be done, and we'll simplify others until they are more fun than work. And we'll plan our time and tasks so that we can enjoy the garden more.

The book is divided into twelve chapters—one for each month. Start at the current month, if you prefer. If it is July when you get the book, that's the month to begin with. Each chapter/month is virtually self-sufficient, although you will find frequent cross-references telling you where additional information may be found in other chapters.

If you've never mulched, fertilized, or pinched back, don't worry. Scattered throughout the book are "boxes" telling you how to do these various gardening arts—they are listed in the table of contents. When you're called upon to perform these tasks, we tell you where to find the box that tells you how. There are also special boxes on categories of plants, such as white gardens or ground covers.

In addition, there are flower recipes. A surprising number of flowers are edible, or may be used as seasoning or garnishes. If you like to nibble roasted sunflower seeds, for instance, the April chapter tells you how to raise, dry, and roast them. Some plants will last the whole year, if you know how to dry them. That simple "art" is covered also, in several chapters.

Chapter sections are: *Plant of the Month, Do It Now, Let's Get Growing, Other Plantables,* and *Beauty Spots.*

Plant of the Month. This is selected for its long-blooming quality, its variety of form and color, ease of culture, and, in some cases, fragrance and edibility. *Note:* It does not come into bloom in the month where it is featured; rather, it is *planted* that month.

Do It Now. This is concerned with such nonplanting activities as pruning, mulching, dividing, staking—the little things we tend to overlook if we aren't reminded.

Let's Get Growing. Several plants are featured in each month, some more at length than others. If the planting procedure is fairly simple, it is headed **Ground Rules,** and lists such basics as type of soil needed, how much sun (or shade), special watering requirements, if any. Others may be so interesting and so varied in their cultivation that they have the heading **Tips to Make You Tops**, for maximum results.

Other Plantables. This is a list of other things to plant in the month, in addition to those featured in the body of the chapter. Plants in this list are cross-referenced to tell the reader where information may be found elsewhere in the book.

Beauty Spots. These are suggested combinations of flowers for small areas, to add color and excitement to the garden. They are designed for the never-had-a-trowel-in-my-hand-before gardener who needs suggestions about what to plant with what. Compatibility is the key, in these Beauty Spot plantings. The plants of each group have the same requirements as to sun or shade, water, and type of soil, and all are reasonably harmonious as to color, but not stereotyped.

Like any other activity, gardening has a language of its own. And of course it helps to know the language if you're going to communicate with the natives. Gardening terms are explained as we go along, to enable the reader to pick up a smattering of "conversational Gardenese," but there is also a glossary at the back of the book.

As much as possible, common names are used for the plants, rather than botanical or scientific terminology. After all, when was the last time you stopped in at the nursery and asked for a package of *Lathyrus odoratus* seeds, or for a flat of *Antirrhinum majus?* I tried it once, and the nurseryman thought I was speaking a foreign language—which I was, come to think of it; it was Latin, the basis for all those unpronounceable botanical names. Much simpler, isn't it, to ask for nasturtium seeds, rather than *Tropaeolum?* You get waited on faster, too.

There are exceptions, of course, in the matter of plant names. When the botanical name is the one more commonly used—as with *Ageratum,* for instance—that is used in the book, rather than *Floss flower.* And there are cases where, for purposes of clarity, the botanical name is necessary to differentiate between types. After all, if you know three people named Joe, you use their surnames just to keep matters straight.

Here they are, twelve wonderful, flower-filled months, to plan and plant and enjoy. If you will think of the year as a clock, but with months on the dial, instead of hours, you and your plants can have the time of your lives. So wind up your clock of the year, and let's get growing!

January

Plant of the Month: Gaillardia. Colorful, early-flowering, long-blooming, it flourishes in the hottest of the hot weather, and is drought tolerant. It is also a long-lasting cut flower. Its vivid colors, reminiscent of Indian blankets, account for its other names, Blanket Flower and Indian Blanket.

January

The Start-Something Month

Now is the time for planning, planting, and pruning.

Janus, "god of the beginning of things," gave his name to January (courtesy of the Romans).

And it's pretty appropriate, since this beginning-of-the-year month has a tremendous number of plants eager to start growing for Southern California gardeners.

With the excitement and distractions of the holidays past, it's time to turn your attention to spring-blooming bulbs, bedding plants and seeds for spring and summer bloom, azaleas for years of glorious color—in short, this is one of the greatest planting months of the year.

It's also time for fertilizing winter bloomers, pruning roses, and planning special combinations of plants to vary the established garden and fill in bare spaces in new ones.

DO IT NOW

Keep alert to frost warnings on radio and television weather forecasts. Marguerites and felicias are vulnerable to a cold snap, azalea buds can be damaged for the rest of the year, and cinerarias can be killed off. If your area is due for a drop in temperature, protect young, tender plants at night with some overhead covering such as newspapers or plastic bags. (But be sure to remove the coverings before the sun comes out, to avoid a destructive buildup of heat.)

Feed winter bloomers such as calendulas, cyclamen, pansies, petunias, stocks, and violets. They are not getting the nitrogen they need, because soil bacteria that release nitrogen are dormant now. Help the blooming things along with organic fish fertilizer. (See **The Art of Fertilizing,** *March.*)

Azaleas and Camellias

These plants are two exceptions to the matter of feeding winter bloomers. Their mealtime months are March, May, and August. (We'll remind you when the time comes.) That's the schedule recommended by the experts at Descanso Gardens in La Canada, one of the world's great gardens.

Camellia blossoms should be picked off as soon as they begin to fade, and fallen blossoms should be removed from the ground. This is the best way to cope with and limit the spread of petal blight, a fungus disease that shows up as small brown spots on the petals and a dark, mushy look at the center of the flower. Don't throw the blossoms on the compost heap, if you have one. (*See* **The Art of Composting,** *September.*) Rather, toss them into the trash can.

Petal blight has two cycles: in the opening bud and in the fallen flower. So keep the camellia blossoms picked off and picked up, or the cycles could petal all around your garden!

Roses

Spray roses this month with a dormant spray. It will get rid of any pests wintering in the plant. (See **The Art of Pest Control,** *March.*)

It's time to prune roses, too, in the coastal and inner coastal sections. If you live in the interior valleys, this can wait until February.

Pruning isn't such a thorny problem as you might think. Here are the three basic

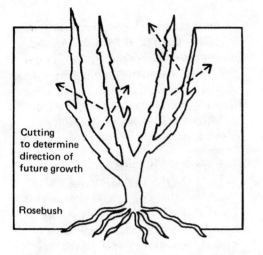

Cutting
to determine
direction of
future growth

Rosebush

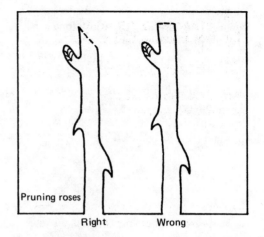

Pruning roses

Right   Wrong

reasons for pruning:

1. to get rid of damaged or excess wood;
2. to increase bloom;
3. to improve the shape of the plant.

Here's what you need in addition to the plant:

☐ a pair of heavy garden gloves with long cuffs to protect your arms against scratches;
☐ pruning shears;
☐ long-reach shears (4-foot length);
☐ a can of pruning compound.

Follow these basic procedures:

☐ Don't hack; make clean cuts.
☐ Hold shears so that the cutting blade is at the bottom; this avoids crushing or tearing the wood.
☐ Have shears clean and sharp. Dull ones can damage the wood.
☐ Before you cut, decide which direction you want new growth to go: if to the right, look for a leaf bud on that side, and cut in that direction (see above, left).
☐ Cut on a slant, about a quarter of an inch above the bud. A slanted surface sheds water quickly and prevents it from seeping into the wood (see above, right).
☐ Use pruning compound to seal any cut

more than half an inch in diameter. Otherwise, bacteria or fungi can get into the fresh cut, or boring insects can move in and lay their eggs.

Here are the simplified methods of pruning roses.

Floribundas. Prune lightly, taking off no more than a quarter of last year's growth, which will be slightly lighter in color than the older wood, and will angle out from a point just below the previous cut.

Grandifloras. These, too, can do with very little pruning, because of their natural sturdiness and vigor. Cut back no more than half of last year's growth.

Hybrid Teas. On the strong, vigorous bushes, remove some of the basal canes (conversational Gardenese for the wood growing at base of the plant), just enough to make the plant look balanced. Leave from five to seven canes—but cut them back to half of the previous year's growth. On the weaker, less vigorous-looking bushes, leave from five to seven canes, but cut these back to 2 feet in height.

Climbing Hybrid Teas. These should not be pruned until they are three years old, except for removal of dead wood and canes crossing other canes. When they are old enough, remove some of the old canes, but leave one new cane for each old one removed. An easy way to remove long canes is to cut them in three places, then draw the pieces down rather than pulling them out.

Tree Roses. Cut back just far enough to leave from one to three leaf buds on last year's growth. Cut TO outside buds, to maintain the full, rounded look.

LET'S GET GROWING

Azaleas

These are in bloom at the nurseries so now is the ideal time to select the colors you like. With the right choice of early and late bloomers, you can arrange to have nine months of azalea color in your garden.

Here are some varieties to consider (months listed are those in which the plants are in bloom):

January to March
Southern Indica
   George Tabor, orchid, single; Glory of Sunninghill, orange-red, single; Formosa, lavender, single.
Kurume
   Hino-crimson, red, single; Laughing Water, single, red.
Rutherfordiana
   Albion, white, hose-in-hose (conversational Gardenese for double flowers giving the appearance of one growing inside the other); L. J. Bobbink, orchid, hose-in-hose; Rose Queen, pink, semidouble.
March to May
Mossholder Gold Cup Hybrids
   Sun Valley, white, double.
Southern Indica
   Pride of Dorking, red, single.
September to December
Rutherfordiana
   Rose Queen, pink, semidouble.

Kurume
   Coral Bells, coral, hose-in-hose.
Mossholder Gold Cup Hybrids
   Desert Rose, salmon, single.

Tips to Make You Tops with Azaleas
1. Make the hole roughly 2 feet wide, foot deep, in a partially shaded location.
2. Mix compost (see **The Art of Composting,** *September)* or leaf mold in with the soil, but use peat moss in the area immediately surrounding the roots. Peat moss has good water-holding properties and also gives the acid reaction so important to azaleas.
3. Fill the hole with water and let it soak in. Be sure the peat moss is well soaked. Set the plant in the center of the hole, adding the planting mixture so that the crown of the plant (*crown:* conversational Gardenese for the section between root and stalk) will be slightly above the surface to allow for settling. Set too low, it will not have proper drainage.
4. Firm the planting medium and water well again.

Bulbs for Spring Bloom

Bring out the hyacinth and tulip bulbs you bought last fall and stored in the refrigerator. The six or eight weeks' cooling period has provided an artificial winter to compensate for our mild winters that don't allow for a normal time of dormancy.

There is a rule of thumb (green, of course!) that calls for planting bulbs at a depth equal to two-and-a-half times their circumference. But that's too general for *all* types. Amaryllis, for instance, must be planted with the tip of the bulb just showing *above* the soil surface. The Madonna lily must have its tip 1 inch below the surface. (See **Lilies,** *December.)*

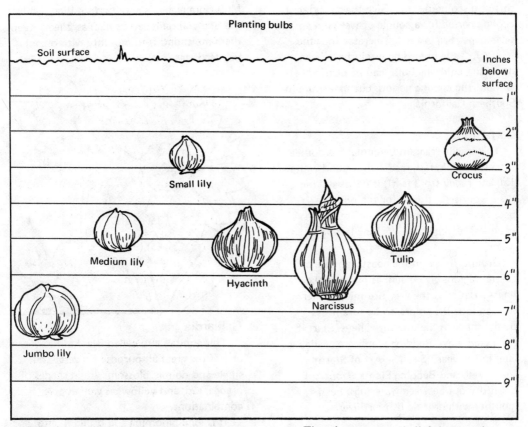

Planting bulbs

Soil surface

Inches below surface

1"

2"

3"
Crocus

Small lily

4"

5"

Medium lily

6"
Hyacinth

Tulip

7"
Narcissus

8"

Jumbo lily

9"

The chart will give you some guidance. Always work the soil deeper (at least a foot) than the actual planting depth for the bulb. Never mix in manure at time of planting, because it may burn the tender bulbs.

Hyacinths. These are easy to grow. Give them sun, although they will grow in partial shade, and a well-drained, rather sandy soil prepared as above and enriched with compost or leaf mold.

Ground Rules. Plant hyacinth bulbs 6 inches deep, 6 inches apart. Don't bother to feed them in their first season of bloom. They come equipped with their own nourishment in the fleshy scales of the bulb. At the end of the first season, they should be given a balanced fertilizer or bone meal. (See **The Art of Fertilizing**, *March.*)

There's a common belief that you just can't give bulbs too much water. Rot! That's what they'll do if you water too heavily before the shoots appear. Keep the bed moist to the touch of your finger, but barely. After the growth starts they want plenty of water, but even then the amount depends on the temperature and the soil texture. (See **The Art of Watering**, *May.*)

Tulips. Prepare the soil as for hyacinths, with plenty of compost or leaf mold. Tulips like sun, but will also grow in partial shade. Plant them 5 inches deep, 6 inches apart. They, too, carry their "food" in the bulb.

It's still not too late to buy tulips and hyacinths, although the choice will be limited and the quality too. Test tulips for firmness at the tip. (See **The Art of Selecting Tulips**, *October.*) Reject any with soft or discolored spots. Give them a brief cooling period for a couple of weeks in an open paper bag in the refrigerator (not the freezer). If the preceding weeks have been unusually cold, the bulbs can be planted without the cooling period, but that's rare in Southern California.

Carnation

This spicily fragrant perennial has double flowers in pink, red, rose, yellow, and white. Tall and rangy (to 3 feet), it needs staking. It's a wonderful flower for the house because its long stems are so adaptable in bouquets, and because it's long-lasting in water.

Ground Rules. In the coastal and inner coastal regions give it sun, as much as six hours a day. But the very hot midsummer sun can fade the colors, so be sure it has partial shade in the interior valleys. Start it from seed, now. Bedding plants are available later in the year. (See **The Art of Starting from Seeds and Bedding Plants,** *January.*) Let it dry out between waterings. Feed monthly with organic fish fertilizer.

Cineraria

This perennial is usually grown as an annual in Southern California. (Many perennials are treated as annuals here because in our mild climate they tend to "bloom themselves out.") Clusters of daisylike flowers in blue, lavender, pink, rose, or white rise from dark green foliage. They are stunning when massed in the various colors.

Ground Rules. Set out the bedding plants now. Cineraria is easily grown from seed, but fall is the time for that.

Cineraria needs a shady or partially shaded location, with loose, loamy soil rich in organic matter. Space the plants about 12 inches apart for an effect of solid color; otherwise, 18 inches apart. One variety,

Multiflora Nana, is about a foot high, while the Star cineraria gets as high as 2 feet. Keep them moist and feed monthly with organic fish fertilizer.

Gaillardia

This annual, also called Blanket Flower, is one of the great all-purpose flowers. The single and double blossoms are in shades of orange, red, and yellow, as well as combinations.

It is long-blooming and drought- and heat-tolerant. Once established in your garden, it will reseed itself industriously. It is a great cut flower. Another of its uses is as a fill-in plant for those blank spaces around a new house.

Ground Rules. Gaillardias grow to a height of about 3 feet, so if planted in borders, they should be at the middle or back of the bed. Space the plants about a foot apart. Start them now from seed, in flats. Later (in March) the bedding plants will be available at the nurseries.

Give gaillardias a rather sandy soil, in full sun. Their watering needs are moderate.

Penstemon

This perennial has spikes of white, pink, red, or lavender flowers. One variety

(Gloxinoides) is about 3 feet tall, but the Blue Bedder penstemon is roughly 12 inches high. Gloxinoides has a wide range of colors, just about every one except blue and yellow. Blue Bedder has blue and light purple flowers.

Ground Rules. Penstemon demands a light, sandy, well-drained soil, because excess moisture, as in heavy, poorly drained soil, will cause root rot. Give it at least half a day of sun in the coastal and inner coastal areas, but partial shade in the hot, inland sections.

Here's a tip: Cut the plants back after flowering (cut back to about half height), and they will reward you with another round of bloom. They are easily propagated by stem cuttings. (See **The Art of Propagation from Softwood Cuttings,** *March.*)

Primrose, English

There's really nothing prim about the primrose. The colors are bold, dashing purple, red, pink, ivory, and orange-to-copper, all with a splash of yellow at the center of the flower. This one is really a "perennial favorite." (The annual is Fairy Primrose, not as showy or colorful as the perennial varieties.)

Bedding plants set out now will bloom in spring and well into midsummer. Hot weather will usually terminate the blooming period. Foliage is evergreen, but not particularly decorative after the blossoms are gone.

Tips to Make You Tops with Primroses

1. Soil must be loamy, well drained, and rich in such organic matter as compost, leaf mold, or peat moss.
2. The location must be in full or partial shade, depending on summer temperatures in your location.
3. Adequate moisture for primroses really

means keeping the soil constantly moist.
4. Set the plants a trifle high in the soil, so that water will not settle in the crowns (conversational Gardenese for the area between roots and stem) and soil will not wash over the crowns.
5. Mulch with compost, leaf mold, or peat moss, to keep the roots cool and moist. Two inches of mulch spread on the surface of the planting area will do it. (See **The Art of Mulching,** *February.*)
6. Feed once a month with a low-nitrogen fish fertilizer.
7. When the plants become crowded, divide them after the blooming period ends, around June.
8. To divide: Loosen the soil around the outer edges with a trowel or spading fork and lift the whole clump. Pull apart gently. Plant the new divisions in the same type of well-drained, humusy soil recommended in Paragraph 1. As suggested in Paragraph 4, set them a bit high.

Verbena, Garden

This is a perennial treated as an annual. The solid, compact blooms are blue, pink, purple, red, or white. Verbena is drought-resistant, so it thrives in hot-summer climates, but does well also in the cool-summer areas.

Ground Rules. Give it full sun and practically any kind of soil. It can do with very little water. Start the seeds now, in flats; transplant when night temperatures are remaining above 50 degrees. Or buy the bedding plants in March.

This is the most adaptable of the verbenas. It grows to about 12 inches in height and is attractive in beds or rock gardens, either massed or used to give just a splash of color here and there. Space the plants 6 inches apart for solid color effects or 10 inches apart as color accents.

THE ART OF STARTING FROM SEEDS AND BEDDING PLANTS

It takes longer to grow your plants from seed, of course, than to start out with bedding plants bought from the nursery. But in addition to the fact that seeds cost less than bedding plants, there is nothing that can surpass that green and magic moment when *a seed you planted* nudges its way up through the soil!

Bedding plants, on the other hand, give you an almost instant garden. Some will be already in bud or bloom in the flats, and if you buy the more mature plants, in 4-inch pots or gallon cans, you really have a head start, and in the case of perennials, you are set for several years. There are advantages to both sides.

Tips to Make You Tops with Seeds and Bedding Plants

1. Buy your seeds at the nursery or garden supply center where you can get whatever else you need in the way of tools, containers, and planting mixture. Later on you may want to study seed catalogs. Or you may want to save and plant seeds from your own garden. But the advantage of starting with seeds grown by professional seedsmen is that they are from specially selected stock, and many are bred to be resistant to disease.

2. Planting seeds directly into the ground where you want them to grow sounds easier than starting them in containers, but even for hardy seeds that don't need to be started in containers and then transplanted, there are advan-

tages to the container method: (a) You have control over sun and moisture. (b) You protect them from hungry pests.

3. Containers—buy, borrow, or make your own

□ *Flats* are square or oblong shallow boxes of various sizes, but usually 3 inches deep. Some nurseries give away their 12-inch-square plastic flats when they have finished with them.

□ *Bulb pans* or *flowerpots* can be used if you are not planting large amounts of seed.

□ Save and reuse the plastic *pony packs* you buy bedding plants in at nurseries. I have a plastic tray which holds eight pony packs and find this the ideal set-up for planting a variety of seeds. The tray makes for easy handling.

□ Half-gallon *milk cartons* cut lengthwise make two containers roughly the size of pony packs. Fasten the end where the pouring spout is with staples, and poke six or eight small holes in the bottom for drainage.

4. Scrub any containers you are recycling, and dry them in the sun. This is a protection against any insect pests or diseases left over from previous "tenants."

5. Put a few bits of broken clay pots (called crocks) or pebbles, in the bottom of the container to facilitate drainage by keeping the holes unclogged yet prevent soil from being washed away.

6. For a planting medium, the simplest thing to do is to buy a

commercial mixture called "potting mix." This has the advantage of being sterile. If you want to mix your own, use one-third garden soil, one-third sand, one-third peat moss or screened compost. (Sift the compost through a coarse screen to remove coarser bits of material.)

7. Fill the container to within half an inch of the rim. Moisten, but not to the point of sogginess.

8. Follow the directions on the seed packet as to planting depth. A good general rule is to plant twice as deep as the diameter of the seed.

9. *Fine seeds.* Scatter them over the surface, then gently press with the palm of your hand or a flat tool. It is not necessary to cover them; they will slip into the planting mixture.

10. *Medium-sized seeds*—shake out of the envelope, into the row, cover and water gently.

11. *Large seeds.* Same as 10, except seeds are set in place individually. Cover, and water gently. I use a sprinkler bottle—the old-fashioned kind used to sprinkle clothes for ironing. It's gentle enough not to wash the soil off the seeds.

12. Set the containers in a sheltered spot, out of direct sun. Keep them moist, but just barely.

13. As soon as the first green shoots are up, they will need plenty of light, but direct sun will dry them out too fast. Keep them comfortably moist. If they once dry out, they will stop developing and you might as well throw out the whole batch. Too much moisture can cause rot, or that bug-a-boo of the seedling set, *damping-off.* That's conversational Gardenese for a fungus disease that causes the plants to rot at the soil level. Overwatering and poor air circulation are the villains. (Cheer up! Once the seedlings have their true leaves, the danger is past. I have never lost a batch yet, and I think it is because I don't follow the common procedure of covering the container with newspaper or a pane of glass, which can impede air circulation.)

14. When the seedlings are about an inch high, thin them. First moisten the soil so the roots will come up easily, then remove and discard the excess seedlings so that those remaining will not quite touch each other.

15. The first set of leaves are called "seed leaves," and look nothing at all like the "true leaves" which succeed them. When the second set of true leaves appears, the seedlings may be "lifted" or "pricked out." Have another container ready, with a slightly more substantial planting mixture, such as garden soil and screened compost, or just the soil alone. Gently lift the seedling up and out by sliding a spoon handle or a tongue depressor into the soil. (I often

skip this intermediate step, and have never found that my seedlings had any less vigor for growing in crowded quarters, until ready for transplanting.)

16. When the seedlings are ready for transplanting in their permanent home, I begin giving them a couple of hours a day of direct sun for several days, to get them acclimated. (But no hot noonday sun.)

17. Prepare the bed several days in advance. Dig the soil to a depth of 12 inches, turn and pulverize the clods. Rake smooth. Add 2 or 3 inches of compost over the whole surface and dig it in well. Add bone meal or super-phosphate—about 2 1/2 pounds to a bed 5 feet by 40 feet. Work that in well, also. Water down and let it settle.

18. Late afternoon is the ideal transplanting time. In this way, seedlings are not subjected to wilting by the sun. Of course any time of day in foggy, overcast weather is good for transplanting.

19. Lift the plants from the container with a putty knife or any flat, narrow tool. This helps to keep the soil from falling away from the roots. Insert the tool on four sides of the seedling to form a cube, or take up several seedlings in one cube, and gently pull apart. Water the planting hole before setting the plant in. Then fill in around the plant with the soil, and water gently so that the soil falls in closely around the roots. (This is a better method than that of pressing the soil in with your hands.)

20. About a week later, pinch back the seedlings. (See **The Art of Pinching Back**, *April*.) This is the practice of pinching off—yes, actually, with thumb and forefinger—the stem section just above the top set of leaves. What happens then? Wonderful things! The energy that would be centered in that one stem will now be distributed to the other parts of the plant. Result: more flowers, bushier plants.

Bedding Plants

Steps 17 through 19 are applicable to setting out bedding plants you buy at the nursery. Bedding plants are, after all, just seedlings grown bigger. When buying bedding plants, select those with sturdy stems and healthy-looking foliage (not drooping or with yellowed or spotted, diseased-looking leaves). The tall, spindly plants have been left in the flats too long.

Seeds Sown in Ground. Handle the same way, up through # 11. When the seedlings are between 2 and 3 inches high, thin by transplanting (most seed packets will give directions as to proper spacing), to allow the remaining plants to have adequate growing room for their size when mature. Utilize the seedlings removed at this point to expand the bed, or set them out elsewhere.

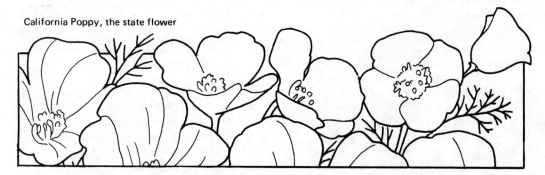

California Poppy, the state flower

FOUR BEAUTY SPOTS FOR JANUARY PLANTING

Webster's defines a *beauty spot* as "a patch or spot put on the face to heighten the beauty by contrast." You can do the same thing through beauty spots on the face of the garden. Here are four plantings to try, all with similar sun, soil and water needs. Try these or work out others and be your own landscape artist!

NAME	HEIGHT (INCHES) & SUGGESTED COLORS	SUN/SHADE	SOIL
Seeds:			
Calendula	12-18, yellow, orange	Full sun	Any
Lobelia	6, blue	Full sun	Fertile
Seeds:			
Oriental Poppy	24-36, red with black center	Sun	Well drained
Matilija Poppy	24-36, white	Sun	Well drained
Seeds:			
For a "scents-ible" combination, try these fragrant ones:			
Heliotrope	12-20, deep purple	Sun	Loamy
Mignonette	12, deep yellow	Sun	Loamy
Petunia (dwarf single)	9, white, pink	Sun	Average
Sweet Alyssum ("Violet Queen")	6, violet	Sun	Average
Bedding Plants:			
For an instant, or almost, Beauty Spot, try these bedding plants:			
Gerbera (Transvaal Daisy)	12-18, mixed (cream, salmon, yellow)	Sun, light shade	Well drained, loamy
Perennial Candytuft	6-10, white	Sun, light shade	Well drained, loamy

OTHER PLANTABLES FOR JANUARY

Here are additional plants that may be started this month. The planting information will be found in the chapters indicated below by month. Unless otherwise shown, reference is to "Let's Get Growing" section.

SEEDS

Bells-of-Ireland	*June*	Hollyhock	*February*
Calendula	*August, November;* also *September* "Beauty Spots"	Osteospermum	*November*
		Painted Tongue	*June* "Beauty Spots"
California Poppy	*September, November* "Beauty Spots"	Pansy	*October, July;* also *March* "Beauty Spots"
Clarkia	*September*	Snapdragon	*September*
Columbine	*February* "Beauty Spots"	Stock	*August, July;* also *September* and *October* "Beauty Spots"
Delphinium	*February*		
English Daisy	*February* "Beauty Spots"		
Forget-me-not	*March* "Beauty Spots"	Sweet Alyssum	*August, September, November;* also, *January* "Beauty Spots"
Godetia	*February* "Beauty Spots"		

BEDDING PLANTS

Calendula	*August, November;* *September* "Beauty Spots"	Delphinium	*February, April, July*
		Foxglove	*August*
Candytuft, perennial	*May, November, August*	Osteospermum	*November*
Columbine	*February* "Beauty Spots"	Pansy	*October, July;* also *March* "Beauty Spots"
Coral Bells	*July, September;* also *June* "Beauty Spots"	Snapdragon	*September*

BULBS

Calla Lily	*February*	Lily	*December*
Daffodil	*October*	Lily-of-the-valley	*February*
Gladiola	*February, May, November*		

February

Plant of the Month: Hollyhock. Reaching us from England by way of China, this one has been beautifying America's gardens since the sixteenth century. Plant in rows beside a wall or a picket fence, or in informal groups near porch or patio entrance.

February

The Clean Up, Sort Out, Tool Up Month

"I heard the footfall of the flower spring . . ."—Sappho

Spring is getting ready to make a grand entrance, so get your creative energies going. The Roman name for this month comes from the word *februare,* meaning "to purify," and that's a good watchword for the garden. It reminds us to get at the cleaning-up and clearing-out jobs, such as readying garden tools and sorting out flats and other containers. February is one of the best months for starting seeds in containers, to get a head start on flooding the garden with spring color. (See **The Art of Starting from Seeds and Bedding Plants,** *January.*) For inland gardeners it's the month to start cool-weather annuals, in order to provide a long season of bloom before the summer heat discourages them. Inland gardeners should also prune roses now. (See **Roses,** *January.*)

While you're doing these "purifying" jobs, don't forget those areas where debris may have accumulated over the winter months. Stacks of flower pots or other containers, piles of firewood, drifts of last year's leaves under the shrubbery—all make snug hiding places for snails and insect pests.

It's the last month to use dormant sprays to get rid of pests and diseases that may be spending the winter in the garden. But remember—*dormant sprays are for deciduous plants only* (*deciduous* is conversational Gardenese for plants that shed their leaves), and can injure foliage of other plants. If you spray your roses, follow container directions carefully and cover nearby evergreen plants. (See **The Art of Pest Control,** *March.*)

Weeding is important anytime, but especially now. The winter rains have given weeds a head start in moist soil that welcomes any seed. The winds of March will be coming along soon to scatter them in greater quantity and variety.

DO IT NOW

Roses

Now is the time to feed them. Who would believe anything so elegant could be so greedy? They should be fed every month from now until September. Organic fish fertilizer is good, or any commercial rose food. If you use the latter, it will probably be in dry form. Soak the ground thoroughly before and after applying the food. This helps to hurry the nutrients on their way to the root zone. (See **The Art of Fertilizing,** *March.*)

Make a bowl for the "food" by heaping the soil in a circle around the plant, forming a shallow basin about 18 inches across. This keeps the granules of food from being washed away by rain or irrigation.

This is also a good time to mulch roses. Use steer manure or compost. Apply the mulch to the thickness of an inch or two. Mulching need not interfere with the feeding, incidentally; simply draw the mulch back with a rake or with whatever tool works best for you; apply the fertilizer, and then replace the mulch.

LET'S GET GROWING

Calla Lily

February is the time to plant callas—the traditional tall white, the pink, and the yellow. The pink and the yellow are dwarf varieties, differing from the white not in color and size but in the need for sun. The

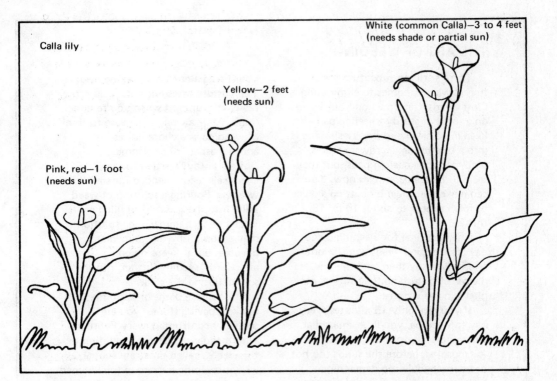

Calla lily

Pink, red—1 foot
(needs sun)

Yellow—2 feet
(needs sun)

White (common Calla)—3 to 4 feet
(needs shade or partial sun)

pink grows to 1 foot, the yellow to 2 feet, the white to 3 or 4 feet.

Ground Rules. *White:* Plant in partial shade in the coastal and inner coastal sections; full shade in the hot interiors. *Pink, yellow:* Full sun in coastal and inner coastal areas; partial shade in the hot interiors.

Plant the rhizomes (conversational Gardenese for the elongated, swollen underground stem) about 2 inches deep, with the eyes up. The pink should be set 6 inches apart, the yellow and the white 12 inches apart. They will grow in average soil, but adding compost or leaf mold always improves drainage. Water no oftener than once a week until new shoots are up. From then on, keep the ground moist.

Delphinium

The California hybrids of this stunning perennial, Pacific Giants (also called candle delphinium), reach a height of 8 feet. However, if you want a smaller plant, try the more delicate Chinese or Siberian delphinium, also called larkspur. They grow from 12 to 18 inches high, although the blossoms are not as spectacular as those on the giants. An intermediate size is the Garland delphinium, with Belladonna and Bellamosum being the most commonly grown.

Tips to Make You Tops with Delphiniums

1. Delphiniums need a rich soil, worked as deep as 2 feet, augmented with compost or bone meal, up to one cup per plant. Give them full sun in the coastal and inner coastal areas, but partial shade in the interior valleys.

2. Watering techniques are specialized. Avoid letting water settle in the crown (conversational Gardenese for that portion of the plant between the root

THE ART OF WEEDING

There's still no substitute for fingers when it comes to eliminating most weeds. Get down on your knees on a soft but sturdy kneeling pad—I keep mine clean and dry by slipping it into a plastic bag. Hardware stores used to stock kneeling pads, but they seem to be scarce articles now. You can make your own by cutting a piece of foam rubber to about 10 by 18 inches.

The best time for weeding is the day after a rain. Weeds will slip out relatively easily then, and there is less danger of disturbing the roots of other plants in the vicinity.

If you give only 15 minutes every day to weeding, you'll be amazed at what you accomplish. Try it early in the morning, before the sun is too hot or your schedule too demanding.

It's a great time for thinking, too. There's a bit of Thoreau in all of us, and every garden is a potential Walden. Weeding time is pretty sure to be a time of solitude, even if you have a houseful of family. Just the announcement that you're going to weed the garden will usually guarantee your being alone. It's relaxing, too. The posture eases tensions—you can't really stay uptight when you're down loose. After a while you cease to think of weeding as a chore but as just another aspect of gardening.

I am always startled to see chemicals recommended for simple weeding. Pouring a solution of weed killer into the soil is like killing gnats with a sledgehammer. The solution may accomplish your immediate purpose, but it keeps on going afterwards, seeping further into the soil, polluting the area.

If you have paths or patio made of brick or paving stones, you are probably confronted every February with maddening bits of vegetation in the cracks, called prostrate spurge, as well as creeping buttercup (nicknamed "sitfast," and no wonder!), and chickweed.

Plucking them out by hand is a long, monotonous job. By the time you pull them up, you may be as prostrate as the spurge. A simple remedy that demands no muscle or chemicals is to mix 8 ounces (1 cup)

and the stem) as this can cause rot. It's better to irrigate—that is, water at ground level—than to do direct or overhead watering. (See **The Art of Watering**, *May*.)

3. After cutting the flower, bend the stalk so that it won't channel water down to the crown. (The stalk is hollow.)

4. The taller delphiniums must be staked. Do it when you first set the plants out, putting the stake in first, then the plant, about an inch from the stake. (See **The Art of Staking**, *April*.)

5. Use a balanced fertilizer such as 5-10-5, when the young plants are about half grown, before the buds appear. (See **The Art of Fertilizing**, *March*.)

6. To get a blooming bonus in the fall, cut off the summer blooms as soon as they fade. New shoots will come up at the

of table salt in a half gallon of hot water, and pour it in the cracks in sufficient quantity to soak the roots of the weeds. (This solution should not be used in other parts of the garden, since salts build up in our Southern California soil as it is.)

Three tools to simplify weeding are the dandelion digger, the plantain extractor, and the scuffle hoe (or

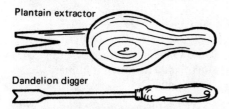

Plantain extractor

Dandelion digger

Dutch hoe). The dandelion digger is useful in reaching deep and cutting long roots.

The plantain extractor gets under the flat leaves of the plantain; then, as you rock it back on its rounded sides, it simply lifts the multirooted pest. It's equally good for dandelions. In fact, both of these tools are useful for a wide variety of weeding jobs.

Scuffle hoe (or Dutch hoe)

The scuffle hoe has a straight, flat, double-edged blade; it is used with a back-and-forth movement to loosen surface soil and remove weeds. (Watch it, though, when you get close to the plant.) The traditional garden hoe should be avoided. It can do more harm than good around tender plants.

Traditional hoe (don't use)

base of the plant. When they are about 6 inches high, cut the old stalk all the way to the ground. In this way, all the energy that might have gone into producing seeds when the flowers faded is redirected into new growth.

7. Are you a plant nibbler? As you work in the garden, do you chew on a stem or leaf? DON'T nibble delphiniums. Leaves and stems are poisonous.

Gladiola

Now is the time to give the garden a glad hand. Because of their diversity of color and range in size, there is scarcely a place in the garden where gladiolas won't fit in.

Before we go any further, let's deal with the matter of nomenclature, singular and plural. Which is it—gladiola/gladiolas; gladiolus/gladioli; gladiolus/gladioluses? My preference is for gladiola/gladiolas.

THE ART OF MULCHING

A mulch is a layer of material spread on the surface of the soil, around a plant. Usually it is between 1 and 2 inches thick. The purpose of a mulch is to keep roots cool and moist, prevent the surface soil from compacting and crusting, discourage weeds, and add organic matter to the soil. Because it is absorbent, it also conserves water, so there is less runoff (loss of soil through heavy rains or watering). The best mulching materials are compost, leaf mold, or ground fir bark. Sawdust is sometimes recommended, but the soil bacteria that break it down consume so much nitrogen in the process that plants may be left temporarily short of that valuable substance. Shredded newspapers are perfectly adequate as a mulch, but look messy and have a tendency to mat down after the rains.

Peat moss is an excellent soil conditioner if worked into the soil before you plant. It makes for good drainage because it's fibrous and breaks down slowly; thus it improves the tilth (conversational Gardenese for *structure*) of the soil. Used as a mulch, however, it requires careful handling. It must be kept moist; once dried out, it becomes water repellent.

As a matter of fact, few things can be more baffling for the new-to-it-all gardener than peat moss. The name implies something moist and manageable; instead, here we are with a bag full of light, dry, fluffy STUFF as hard to handle as feathers. Stop right there! You don't use it in *that* condition.

Place it in a good-sized container (it will expand considerably when completely moistened) and pour water into the center and then around the edges. Stir it occasionally to distribute the moisture, and add water as necessary. Let it sit a day or so until it has completely absorbed the water.

Anyway, this is the time to plant whatever-you-call-'ems.

From planting time to blossom time is 90 to 110 days, so you will have them glorifying the garden by the middle of May.

Tips to Make You Tops with Gladiolas

1. Planted now, they will bloom while our weather is still on the cool side, so give them full sun (at least five hours). Later plantings, timed for midsummer and early fall blooming, should have partial shade.

2. Give gladiolas a rather sandy soil, with sufficient organic matter added to give support to the tall spikes when they are heavy with bloom. Choose your soil and space carefully; gladiolas just won't compete for nutrients with large shrubs and trees.

3. Dig an 8-inch hole, about 4 inches in diameter, for each corm. (While gladiolas are corms, they are classed with bulbs, and the two words are often used interchangeably. A corm is an underground stem resembling a bulb, but without scales.) In the bottom of the hole put a handful of bone meal. The lighter the soil, the

deeper the corm should be planted. Set small ones 3 to 4 inches deep; larger ones as deep as 6 inches.

4. Place the stakes in the hole before you set the corms in. Five-foot stakes will be about right for taller varieties.

5. For a progression of bloom, stagger the plantings two weeks apart, *but don't plant after June.* The quality seems to deteriorate in direct proportion to lateness of bloom.

6. Once planted, the corms must not dry out. But use discretion in watering since too much can cause rot. Later, during the budding and blooming period, they will need to be kept moist.

7. To avoid winding up with sad glads, rotate your "crops." Gladiolas use up the soil nutrients after five or six years in one place.

8. When the bloom period is over, let the foliage turn yellow. Then dig up the corms. Loosen the soil with a spading fork, and then lift the corms out and gently shake them free of dirt. *Now* cut the foliage back, to within about half an inch of the top of the corm.

9. A new corm will be attached to the old one. Don't separate the two until they have dried out. Spread them on a flat surface, preferably in the sun. When they have dried out enough for the old corms to be detached easily (tug gently to test), discard them.

10. Sprinkle with a commercial bulb dust, just enough to coat them lightly (about a teaspoonful to eight or ten corms). This will protect them against disease and pests in the dormant period. (Gladiolas must have a dormant time of at least eight weeks.)

11. Store the young corms in paper bags (open at top for ventilation) in a cool, dry place such as the garage, toolhouse, or basement.

Hollyhock

Don't overlook this biennial, although that would be a physical impossibility since it grows to a height of 9 feet or more. Few plants surpass it for distinctiveness of form and a kind of stately demureness. Color range includes pale pink, lavender, yellow, and deep, almost black red. The singles, more typical of colonial gardens, are to me the most beautiful, but the doubles and semidoubles are lovely, too.

Hollyhock doesn't combine too effectively with other plants, because its distinctive style doesn't blend well. Also, it needs open space around it—too much shade and crowding have a bad effect on the foliage. All the colors harmonize, and a combination of the various singles, doubles, and semidoubles with a wall or fence as background is spectacular.

The seed does not reproduce dependably. I save mine anyway (each stalk produces a tremendous number of seeds) and plant every year in order to have an annual stand, since the life span of a biennial is only two years. Planting from homegrown seed is like dipping your hand into nature's grab bag.

Ground Rules. If night temperatures are still dropping below 50 degrees, start the hollyhock seed in flats and transplant the seedlings when they are about three weeks old. Otherwise, sow seeds directly into the ground. If you moisten the planting medium and slip the container into a plastic bag (close the bag by tucking the end under the container), it will make a greenhouse atmosphere for the seed. But be sure to uncover the plants when the first green tips show.

When setting out the young plants, place them a trifle low in the soil, so that the mature plant will have a good solid foundation. This is a tall plant, so it needs a good firm base. Properly planted, it need not be staked.

Hollyhocks will bloom throughout the summer and into early fall. Water well, about three times a week—oftener when the temperature is running 90 degrees and up. Cut stalks back to the base after the blooming period is over unless you want to save the seeds. In that case, leave the stalks standing until seed casings are dry and brown.

Lily-of-the-Valley

This is a pip of a plant—and that's what the little roots are called—pips. Dormant rootstocks are available at nurseries now. The bell-like white flowers of lily-of-the-valley, on 6-inch stems, are delicate and fragrant. It's a glamorous groundcover in shaded areas, given the rich, moist, humusy conditions it needs. The leaves are coolly beautiful the year round.

Ground Rules. Plant the pips in ı. ɔist, loamy soil; work in plenty of leaf mold, peat moss, or compost. Set them 1 1/2 inches deep and so close that they almost touch. Divisions or clumps should be spaced about 18 inches apart, with the crowns just level with the surface of the soil. These plants give a charming woodland touch when planted under trees or shrubs. Shade and a rich,

moist soil are the two requisites. Under those conditions they may be left undisturbed for years. They are not for the hot interiors, however.

Roses

Whether you are starting a rose garden or adding to the one you have, select bare root stock now, since bare root season ends the first of March. *Bare root* means the plants are bought from the nursery with roots bare of soil, sometimes packed in a small amount of planting medium and wrapped in plastic, or placed in boxes of shavings or sawdust, to keep the roots from drying out.

If they are not wrapped, inspect the roots to see if they appear dried out or if some of the ends are broken. Get the best, the number 1 grade. There is no such thing as a bargain in this matter of selecting roses. And when you get your bare root rose home, don't let it lie around and dry out while you decide where to plant it. Prepare the planting space ahead of time. If you must delay planting, unwrap the plant, put it in a sheltered place out of the sun, and cover the roots with damp soil or compost. Or you can set it in a bucket of water to which you have added rooting hormone.

Ground Rules. Choose the location carefully. Ideally, a rose should have six hours of sun every day, preferably in the morning, and afternoon shade.

Dig a capacious hole, roughly 2 feet deep and 2 feet wide, to allow for the addition of compost or peat moss, well worked in, to combine with the existing soil. The width is doubly important, because rose roots spread out as well as down.

One method of planting is to set the new plant on a cone of soil; that is, form the soil in the center of the hole into a cone-shaped mound and spread the roots outward and downward over it. Although some gardeners believe this is unnecessarily complicated, I

feel it gives support to the plant and leaves fewer air pockets when the hole is filled in. Be sure the bud union (the bulgy-looking place on the main stem) is a good 2 inches *above* (not below) the soil surface. If you are new to Southern California gardening but an old hand with roses, you may think planting the bud union above the surface is some radical new idea—but it's right for Southern California climates. *Below* the surface is for cold winter climates.

Water the hole thoroughly before setting the plant in place. Let the water soak in—through and around the cone. I add more compost and a handful of bone meal just before I set the plant in. Compost helps to make the soil absorbent, yet facilitates good drainage, and bone meal aids root growth. Trim off overlong roots and cut off broken ones at the break. Set the plant on the cone of soil and spread the roots gently over it. Scoop in the mixture of soil and compost, pressing it gently around the roots in order to eliminate air pockets. When the hole has been filled in, press the surface firmly with your foot; put your full weight on it. If the

pressed-down area is a little lower than the surrounding soil surface, so much the better; it will hold moisture better.

It is vital to keep the soil moist until the roots get a good grip on things.

Tips to Make You Tops with Roses

1. The most important thing in caring for roses is proper watering. They need deep watering, which means enough moisture should be applied, slowly, to wet the soil to a depth of 4 to 6 inches.
2. Irrigation (watering at ground level) is preferable to overhead watering. Use a rose bubbler or water wand. (See **Easier Ways to Water,** *June.*)
3. The best time to cut blooms is early in the morning. They will be fresh, dewy, and not jaded by too much heat.
4. Cut blooms just above a five-part leaf. New growth will come quickly from buds at the axil of the leaf (the point where it joins the stem).
5. If you water your roses overhead, or if the lawn sprinklers reach them, be sure it's early enough in the day for the foliage to dry thoroughly before evening.

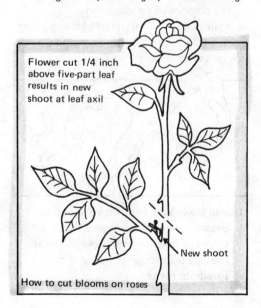

Flower cut 1/4 inch above five-part leaf results in new shoot at leaf axil

New shoot

How to cut blooms on roses

Otherwise you are asking for trouble, such as mildew and black spot.

6. Feed roses with any good commercial rose food or a complete fertilizer such as 5-10-5 once a month from February to September. Water before and after fertilizing.

7. Keep mulched all year long. When applying fertilizer, draw the compost back with a rake, fertilize the soil, then push back into place.

8. To ward off aphids, plant garlic or any member of the onion family near roses.

Sweet Pea

This flower has so much to offer—fragrance, abundance of bloom, an unrivalled color range—that it's worth the special treatment it needs in regard to planting and supporting. The colors are gentle pastels: pink, cream, blue, yellow, lavender; deepening to coral, rose, and scarlet. The long-stemmed blossoms last well in water, making this one of the outstanding cut flowers. Incidentally, the Los Angeles area is considered the ideal sweet pea climate.

It's possible to get immensely complicated in this matter of planting sweet peas, but I use the following simplified method with excellent results:

Tips to Make You Tops with Sweet Peas

1. Soaking the seeds for several hours will soften or split the little jackets. Sweet peas are slow to germinate, and this speeds up the process.

2. Select a sunny location that gets a good flow of air; a humid atmosphere encourages mildew. The soil should be well drained and fairly rich.

3. Dig a trench 18 inches deep, 6 inches wide. Mix the soil with compost or leaf mold, and steer manure. Refill the trench with the mixture to within an inch and a half of the top. (When the seeds are planted 1 inch deep, they will then be in a slight declivity, which helps to keep them moist.)

4. Water the bed and let it settle overnight or for several hours.

5. Plant the seeds 1 inch deep, 1 inch apart. The ground should be kept moist.

6. When seedlings are 2 inches high, thin them to 5 inches apart. You don't get more flowers by crowding a lot of seedlings in a row; you get less—plus mildew.

7. At the time of thinning, set up supports for the vines. Sweet peas will climb as high as 8 feet. To give them a foothold, I use a length of chicken wire with a redwood stake at each end. (After the bloom period is over, I cut down the vines and pull up stakes. The stakes are rolled up in the wire, and the whole apparatus stored until the next planting.)

8. Pinch back the seedlings when they are 3 or 4 inches high. (See **The Art of Pinching Back**, *April.*)

9. NEVER WATER SWEET PEAS OVERHEAD. It will create the mildew-prone environment mentioned above. Irrigate at the base of the plants.

10. Sweet peas will give and give and give—but you must take and take and take. The more you pick, the more flowers will come crowding into bloom. Watch for the seed pods, and pick them off promptly to ensure continuing bloom.

FOUR BEAUTY SPOTS FOR FEBRUARY PLANTING

You can be your own landscape architect! Here are four planting suggestions, including three combinations of plants with similar sun, shade, soil, and moisture needs. These small adventures in the use of color and form are designed to beautify problem areas or to brighten dull sections of the garden. Start with these, then try working out your own designs.

NAME	HEIGHT (INCHES) & SUGGESTED COLORS	SUN/SHADE	SOIL
Seeds:			
Nemesia	10-12, mixed: lavender, pink, yellow, red, white	Full sun	Moist, loamy
Use alone because of the color range.			
Godetia	10, pink, white	Sun, light shade	Average to sandy
Baby Blue Eyes	6, sky blue with white centers	Sun, light shade	Light, well drained
Bedding Plants or 4-Inch Pots:			
Columbine (Rocky Mountain)	30-36, blue and white	Partial shade	Moist, loamy
Primrose, (Juliae hybrids)	8-12, mixed	Partial shade	Moist, loamy
Fern, Maidenhair	12-14	Partial shade	Moist, loamy
This is a planting for cool-summer areas, primarily.			
Bedding Plants:			
English Daisy	6, pink, red, white	Sun, light shade	Moist, loamy
Candytuft, Perennial	6, white	Sun, light shade	Moist, loamy

OTHER PLANTABLES FOR FEBRUARY

Here are additional plants that may be started this month. The planting information will be found in the chapters indicated below by month. Unless otherwise shown, reference is to "Let's Get Growing" section.

SEEDS

Ageratum	*April;* also *March* "Beauty Spots"	Phlox	*May*
Baby's Breath	*July;* also *April* "Beauty Spots"	Shasta Daisy	*May, August;* also *March* "Beauty Spots"
Bells-of-Ireland	*June*	Snapdragon	*September*
Calendula	*August, November*	Stock	*August, July;* also *September* "Beauty Spots"
Forget-me-not	*March* "Beauty Spots"		
Iceland Poppy	*August*	Sweet Alyssum	*August, November*
Larkspur	*May* "Beauty Spots"	Sweet Pea (bush variety)	*October*
Lobelia	*January* "Beauty Spots"		
Mignonette	*January* "Beauty Spots"	Verbena	*January;* also *March* "Beauty Spots"
Painted Tongue	*June* "Beauty Spots"		
Pansy	*October;* also *March* "Beauty Spots"	Wild Flowers	*September*
Petunia	*March;* also *April* "Beauty Spots"		

BEDDING PLANTS

African Daisy (Osteospermum)	*November*	Iceland Poppy	*August*
Calendula	*August, November*	Pansy	*October;* also *March* "Beauty Spots"
Candytuft, perennial	*May, November, August*	Penstemon	*January;* also *April* "Beauty Spots"
Cineraria	*January*	Petunia	*March;* also *April* "Beauty Spots"
Coral Bells	*July, September;* also *June* "Beauty Spots"	Snapdragon	*September*
English Primrose	*January, June;* also *September* "Beauty Spots"	Sweet Pea (bush variety)	*October*
Foxglove	*August*		

BULBS

Amaryllis	*September*	Lilies	*December*

March

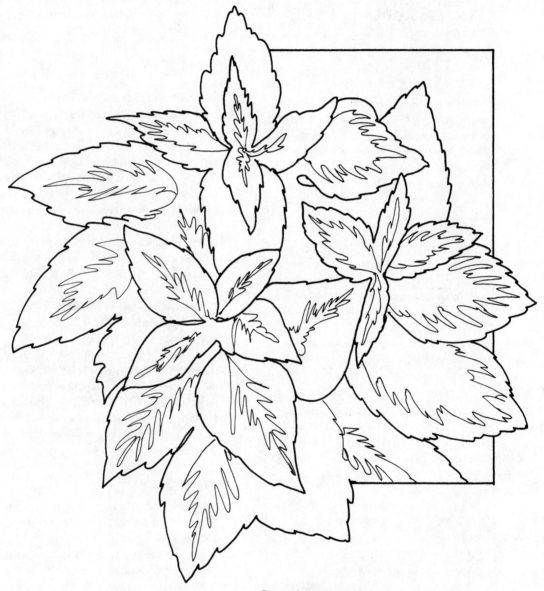

Plant of the Month: Coleus. The belle of the Victorian drawing rooms is returning to popularity! Let its versatile colors light up the garden all summer; then, before the first frost, pot it and bring it in for the winter.

March

Wet or Dry, It's Really Spring

**Plant and feed, but watch
the thermometer.**

This is the time of year when plants can hardly wait to get growing and gardeners can hardly wait to get going—there's so much to plant at this beginning-of-spring-time. Annuals, perennials, bulbs—what a list!

In the ten-month year of the Roman calendar, March was the first month, and it's still a time of great beginnings, gardenwise. But if we are garden-wise, we will keep in mind that some areas in Southern California can still get frost in the early part of the month, so plant and protect accordingly.

March is one of the most important months of the year for fertilizing, because it is the start of the growth season.

If you started a compost heap last fall (see **The Art of Composting,** *September*), the lower sections may be ready now. Scoop

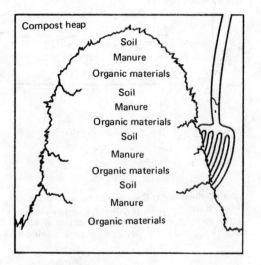

Compost heap

Soil
Manure
Organic materials
Soil
Manure
Organic materials
Soil
Manure
Organic materials
Soil
Manure
Organic materials

some out with a trowel. If it is loamy and loose-textured, almost fine enough to be considered pulverized, it's ready for use. Mix it into the soil as you prepare flower beds or planting holes. Use it as a mulch for such moisture-lovers as begonias, ferns, and primroses.

DO IT NOW

Azaleas and Camellias

These should be given their special food around the middle of this month. (See **The Art of Fertilizing.**) They need a diet with an acid-type reaction, which simply means that our usually alkaline Southern California soil is made more to their liking by the addition of such amendments as cottonseed meal, blood meal, or a good commercial azalea/camellia food. The amount depends on size and height of the plant. (Follow the directions on the package.) Be sure to water before and after feeding. Any fertilizer must be dampened to enter the soil, so this matter of before-and-after watering is important.

Renew the mulch at this time, also. Remove the old mulch if it is over three months old, apply the fertilizer, and then cover with the new mulch. (See **The Art of Mulching,** *February*.) Throw the discarded mulch in the trash in case any insect pests have been wintering in it.

Fuchsia

Fuchsias should be pruned this month. This is so simple that it's fun! Fuchsias bloom on new growth, so get rid of that old, leggy, overhanging wood. Be sure to leave at least two leaf buds on each branch as you trim. As long as you do that, you can cut the plant back so that it stands no more than a foot high. Weak, spindly-looking branches, however, should be nipped off all the way back to the stem. Save some of the trimmed

THE ART OF FERTILIZING AND SOIL IMPROVEMENT

When a plant is setting buds, for example (*setting buds:* conversational Gardenese for developing flower buds), a low-nitrogen or "bloom fertilizer" will be recommended. The label may read 2-5-5, meaning "2 percent nitrogen, 5 percent phosphorus, 5 percent potassium." The remainder is filler—materials to give the fertilizer substance and to separate the nitrogen, phosphorus, and potassium.

To give your plants the proper supplement in their diet, it's important to know what the individual nutrients will do for them. Trying to keep all the separate responsibilities fixed in your mind can be confusing in the early stages.

Here's a simplified system I worked out early in my gardening experience:

Nitrogen. This is the only word of the three with a *g* in it—*g* for Green foliage and Good Growth, for both of which nitrogen is needed.

Are you baffled by the subject? No need to be. Soil must be given supplementary nutrients to make up for those in which it may be deficient. This can be done through the addition of a number of substances—organic matter such as compost and manures, or commercial fertilizers.

As you work with your garden soil, you will come to have a better understanding of its needs. In most Southern California soils, that means some combination of nitrogen, phosphorus, and potassium. A "complete fertilizer" contains all three of these ingredients, not necessarily in equal amounts, but balanced to give the best results for the plant's specific needs. The label will always list the proportions in this order: nitrogen, phosphorus, and potassium.

Phosphorus. Think phonetically here—the dominant sounds are *f, r,* and *s.* Think of *f* for Flower (bloom) development; *r* for Root development; *s* for Seed production. Phosphorus takes care of those departments.

Potassium. The double *s* is the key—for Sturdy Stalks and Stems. Also, potassium increases resistance to fungus disease. (All those *s* sounds!)

When bone meal, for instance, is recommended at time of planting, it is because its principal nutrient is phosphorus, needed for good root development. This is why it is often put into the planting hole before the plant itself.

When you know why you choose a particular fertilizer, it's much easier to keep your plants "fed" properly.

When using organic fish fertilizer, mix it to about half the strength suggested on the label. In that way you won't risk overdosing the plants. If you come on too strong, tender roots can do a slow burn.

Water before and after using organic fish. A good way to apply it is to let it trickle slowly from the container you have mixed it in (it's a concentrate; NEVER use it as it comes from the bottle) and make a circle around the individual plant, about 3 inches from the stalk or crown. (The crown is Gardenese for the section between roots and stalk.)

Why is organic fish fertilizer recommended for so many of the plants in this book? Glad you asked!

☐ It's organic, rather than chemical; therefore, it's nonpolluting.

☐ It releases its nutrients slowly, so the effect is long-lasting.

☐ It's in liquid form and is thus quickly absorbed by the soil.

wood for cuttings, using the tips, shortened to 3 or 4 inches.

Fuchsias growing in hanging baskets require a slightly different pruning technique: Cut the hanging branches back so that they are just long enough to be even with the bottom of the container.

Don't be too rigidly bound by the calendar in garden procedures. It's all right to trim fuchsias earlier than March. If, for instance, we have had one of those Februaries so warm that spring growth is speeded up, run for the clippers.

Start the regular fertilizing schedule for your fuchsias this month—organic fish fertilizer is ideal, used every other week. (Dilute to about half strength for plants in hanging baskets and pots.)

Roses

Roses should be disbudded now if you are going to do it at all. It's strictly a matter of choice. Disbudding is the process of pinching off the side flower buds, leaving just one center bud on the stem. It is standard practice among growers and gardeners who want exhibition-type plants. It simply concentrates the plant's energy into production of a few large blossoms rather than numerous smaller ones. However, it must be done early in the spring (like now), when only a minimum of the plant's energies have gone into bud production.

Be prepared for aphids and thrips to cause problems with your roses. Aphids are easy to see, but the presence of thrips is hard to spot, because it's an inside job. Here you are with a stunning bud ready to open, and what happens? Not a blooming thing! It's a case of arrested development.

The bud will "ball" (conversational Gardenese for remaining unopened) and the edges will brown. Pull the bud open, and at the base of the petals inside you will see innumerable tiny, slender, lemon-colored "nymphs"—the young thrips. (The adults are 1/25th of an inch in length, so you can imagine how tiny the young ones are.)

Use a systemic insecticide, the granule form, for these and other sucking pests. (See **The Art of Pest Control**, below.) Sprinkle the insecticide on the soil around the plant, water it, and then let nature take its course. The poison will be taken into the plant's system, and any sucking pest will get a lethal dose. Nonsucking insects such as bees and ladybugs are not harmed.

LET'S GET GROWING

Canna

This tropical perennial thrives in the hot interiors and the inner coastal areas, but is averse to the foggy coastal sections.

Be selective in planting this large, determined, restless beauty. It needs plenty of room as the rhizomes (conversational Gardenese for underground stem or rootstock) increase rapidly and the foliage is large. The colors are dominant ones—especially the old-fashioned reds, yellows, and oranges. Hybridizing has produced some softer hues such as coral, pink, salmon, bronze, and white. A circular bed is stunning in a large garden, and a row against a wall is also effective, but it's not an easy plant to use with others.

Tips to Make You Tops with Canna

1. In a sunny location, spade the soil to a depth of 12 to 18 inches. Add about one-half pound of steer manure to a square foot of soil, but delay planting for a week to avoid burning the rhizomes. If the soil is at all heavy, add some organic matter, such as compost (see **The Art of Composting**, *September*) or peat moss, to ensure good drainage,

since cannas will develop bud rot in heavy, badly drained soil.

2. Plant the rhizomes about 5 inches deep, spacing tall varieties (they reach 6 feet) roughly 2 feet apart, dwarf varieties (to 3 feet) about 18 inches apart.

3. Cannas need to be watered well, but the soil should not be soggy. (See **The Art of Watering,** *May.*)

4. Cut back to about 6 inches above ground level in fall, and the evergreen foliage will begin another round. (See *November.*)

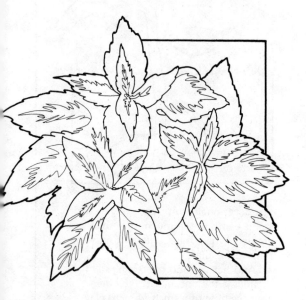

Coleus

This fascinating foliage plant used to be the belle of the drawing room back in Victorian days and is riding the current nostalgia boom back into our hearts and gardens.

Colors come in almost uncountable combinations including ruby red edged with green; maroon and green; white and green; shocking pink with rust and green edging; wine with splotches of yellow and orange.

Tips to Make You Tops with Coleus

1. It needs well-drained soil and partial or full shade. Full sun will make the plants droop and will fade the colors.

2. Start the bedding plants this month as soon as frost danger is past.

3. The real adventure with coleus comes through raising it from seed. Sow the seeds in flats or pony packs this month. (See **The Art of Starting from Seeds and Bedding Plants,** *January.*)

4. When the seedlings are ready for thinning, keep the smaller ones rather than the husky-looking specimens. Oddly enough, the more brilliant colors are produced by the small seedlings; the bigger ones will run to solid green.

5. The plants should be pinched back as often as necessary to keep them bushy and preferably under 2 feet. (See **The Art of Pinching Back,** *April.*) The prunings can be used to start cuttings any time.

6. Remove the tassellike blossoms as soon as they begin to form; otherwise the plant will go to seed and stop producing foliage.

7. Coleus needs to be fed twice a month with organic fish fertilizer.

8. Water regularly, keeping the soil barely moist. A gentle overhead spraying in very hot weather with a misting nozzle or fogger is good for coleuses, but for general watering, apply moisture at ground level.

9. Before the winter rains start or the temperature begins to drop below 45 degrees, pot the plants and bring them indoors for the winter, and they will take their rightful place as perennials. Otherwise, treat them as annuals and start a new batch each year.

10. Mealybugs are the only insect pest to watch for, and these can be removed with a bit of cotton on a toothpick, dipped in rubbing alcohol.

THE ART OF PROPAGATION FROM SOFTWOOD CUTTINGS

March is a good month to start some cuttings of coleus, chrysanthemums, and other softwood plants. (In conversational Gardenese these are plants with soft, or green, stems. It's one way, and a fun way, to increase your garden favorites.)

Some other softwood plants that can be propagated by stem cuttings include begonia, chrysanthemum, dahlia, dianthus, fuchsia, geranium, heliotrope, perennial candytuft, verbena, and vinca.

Cut a 4-inch length of tip growth on a slant, just as in pruning. Remove the leaves or leaf buds on the lower half.

Set cuttings an inch deep in a commercial planting mix or in one you make yourself, such as half sand and half peat moss. The container can be a flat or a flower pot or anything with holes for drainage.

Once the cuttings are in place, water them gently so that the planting mixture will settle evenly. Cuttings should be just far enough apart so that the foliage won't touch.

Make a "greenhouse" by placing a plastic bag over the container and using wire bent into arches to support the plastic. (Wire coat hangers are great for this purpose.) Tuck the ends of the plastic under the container and place your "greenhouse" where it will get warmth and light, but no sun. You will probably not need to water again until it's time to remove the plastic. The air and light can come through the plastic, but moisture does not escape, so an ideal "climate" is created. If you are not sure the moisture is adequate,

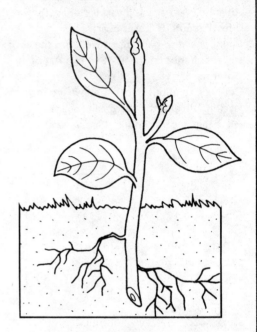

test occasionally with your finger. If soil is damp to the touch, it's moist enough. When you see signs of growth, remove the plastic.

Another method of starting stem cuttings is the pot-in-pot: Plug the drainage hole of a small (4-inch) clay pot with a cork, fill with water, and set it in an 8-inch pot. Fill the space between the large and small pots with the soil mixture, and insert the cuttings in the mixture. The water will seep from the porous sides of the clay pot just gradually enough to keep the planting mixture moist.

Cover with the plastic "tent," just as in the other method. You can check on the root development by removing the water filled inside pot with a gentle twisting motion.

Felicia

Also called Blue Marguerite, this is one of those durable, dependable plants needing little care. Felicia will produce multitudes of blue daisylike flowers with yellow centers well into the fall and sometimes right on through the winter, if the weather is mild.

Tips to Make You Tops with Felicia
1. Give this one full sun, average soil.
2. It's not demanding as to water; a thorough watering a couple of times a week is sufficient.
3. Keep the flowers picked off, to improve appearance and productivity.
4. After the summer blooming period, cut the plant back to 4 or 5 inches in height, and it will reward you with another round of bloom in the fall. Because it's evergreen, it will be attractive even after the bloom period is over.

Marguerite

Also called Paris Daisy, Marguerite is of the same family as felicia—a daisy of another color, but more dramatic since it grows to shrub size, covered with white, yellow, or pink flowers.

Tips to Make You Tops with Marguerite
1. Give it full sun, except in the inland valleys, where it should have partial shade. Bloom will stop when temperatures begin to climb up into the 90s.
2. Prepare the soil with plenty of organic material and keep the plants well watered.
3. For quick color, start with the 4-inch pots or gallon containers, spacing the plants from 2 to 4 feet apart. Bedding plants are available now, also.
4. Keep the faded flowers picked off.
5. Once the blooming period is over, replace with new plants or start some cuttings. Marguerite does not respond to shearing back, so although it is a perennial, it is grown as an annual.

Nasturtium

Plant seeds now to provide a long-lasting splash of color, abundant cut flowers, and tangy additions to salads. It's a perennial but is grown as an annual and will reseed diligently, so that once established it makes a permanent bed or border plant.

Ground Rules. It is so simple to grow and care for that you won't need any "Tips to Make You Tops." Just plant and enjoy it: Half an inch deep, 2 inches apart, thin to 4 inches.

Use the dwarf for bedding or edging. Other types are climbing or trailing. All they ask is sun and space to grow. Average watering, no rich foods, please; if you insist on feeding them, they will simply produce an excessive amount of foliage.

The foliage, incidentally, is one of the attractions of nasturtium. The leaves are shield-shaped and peltate (conversational Gardenese for a leaf that grows on a stem separate from the flower).

Nasturtium colors are yellow, orange, dark red, and pale cherry red; flowers are double as well as single. Not to get too technical about it, single flowers usually have a definite number of uniform petals. Double flowers have many more petals than the single form.

Keep the faded flowers picked off, and the seeds also, unless you are saving the latter for pickles.

Aphids are about the only insect problem, and these can be washed off with a spray-type nozzle.

There is a glamour member of the family—Canary Bird Flower, so called because of its feathery yellow petals. This is a climber, to 15 feet. The leaves are different from the garden nasturtium, with five lobes (segments). Its requirements are different also. It wants a cool summer climate, with a moist, loamy soil. Don't try to grow this one in the hot inland areas.

THE ART OF PEST CONTROL

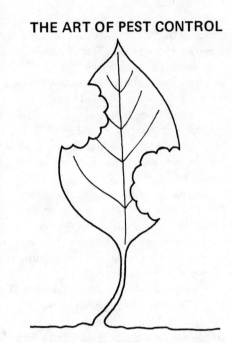

Suckers. Barnum was right; there's one born every minute, or at least it seems that way in the garden. Aphids, leaf hoppers, spider mites, mealybugs, scales, thrips, and white flies suck plant juices from stems, leaves, and flowers.

Some, such as aphids and spider mites, can be washed off with the hose, but others need stronger measures. The hose is only a temporary measure, of course, and large infestations of aphids and spider mites are better handled with systemics.

Snails

Of course sucking insects are just part of the problem. Unfortunately, systemics don't bother snails. These pests are especially plentiful in Southern California, along with slugs, which are shell-less snails. Some wild

and way-out methods of dealing with these pests get into print every now and then, and desperate gardeners scramble to try each one. Here are some of them:

Beer. "See what the boys in the back yard will have . . ." This is frequently lauded as an unbeatable remedy when placed in shallow containers such as pie pans at strategic points around the garden. Maybe I just haven't found the brand they like.

Sandpaper. Collars of sandpaper around plants are advocated to keep the snails and slugs from the plants, the theory being that the pests will not climb over anything abrasive. They not only climbed over the collars I placed around my plants; they ate the glue and the sand right off the paper— and had the plants for dessert.

Wood Ash. This is supposed to act as a repellent when sprinkled around plants, because the snails and slugs dislike the contact. I tried it; it didn't work. They may not have liked the stuff, but they evidently felt it was worth pushing on through to get at the green goodies.

Insecticides

This is the busiest time of year for insects, but reaching for the pesticide is not necessarily the answer. For one thing, many insects build up an immunity to pesticides and this immunity is passed along to succeeding generations. For another, beneficial insects are killed off along with the destructive ones. What happens then is what scientists call a "resurgence." Upon the removal of beneficial insects, destructive ones multiply faster, with fewer predators around to keep them in check. Another side effect is what is called a "secondary outbreak"—the rapid buildup in numbers of a pest that has previously done little damage but that now becomes a serious problem. California pear growers, for example, have found that secondary outbreaks of spider mites almost always follow the chemical control of codling moths.

Soap Spray and "Botanicals"

Soap spray as an alternative to chemical pesticides has its drawbacks, contrary to the glowing recommendations we read. Where the water is hard (that is, with a high lime content), some of the soap is precipitated (separated) by the lime, and rendered much less effective. Also, frequent use of soap sprays may be harmful to foliage.

So don't toast your plants with "Here's suds in your eye!" And don't use laundry detergent if you do make up a batch of soap spray. *Detergents are not soap.* SOAP is soap! Detergents are *really* bad news for your plants.

A group of pesticides, derived from plants and called "botanicals" for that reason, is effective against a number of pests including aphids, thrips, and scale insects. The great advantage to using the botanicals (often called organic insecticides) is that they are nontoxic to humans. Rotenone is one. (Oddly enough, it is toxic to fish; natives of the tropics developed this extract from the root of the derris plant, and used it to

poison fish.) It is available at some nurseries in powdered form.

Pyrethrum, another botanical, is available at nearly all nurseries. It is made from the pulverized flowers of pyrethrum, a variety of chrysanthemum.

Biological Control

Then there is biological control. This is the practice of using beneficial insects to prey on destructive ones. The city of Claremont got rid of the aphids that infested their elms by the purchase of 2 1/4 gallons of ladybugs. One ladybug larva will consume up to 400 aphids in the course of its development to the pupal stage. No wonder they are called "aphid lions"! It is estimated that one ladybug, in its lifetime, eats about 5,000 aphids.

There are at least a dozen companies that raise ladybugs commercially. The Bureau of Entomology of the California Department of Agriculture will furnish addresses on request.

An ounce of prevention is worth a pound of ladybugs, however. Discourage aphids by planting parsley around your roses. Garlic, too, will reduce aphid population, although no one seems to know why. Garlic also increases the fragrance and the vigor of the rose. Any member of the onion family will work, including such ornamentals as golden garlic and giant allium. (See **Giant Allium,** *November.*)

One of the most important things the beginning gardener can add to his or her library is an illustrated book on insects and other pests. That way, you know what to look for.

EAT YOUR PLANT AND HAVE IT TOO: PICKLED NASTURTIUM SEEDS

Nasturtium means "twist of the nose"—not, as you might think, because of its spicy aroma, but because centuries ago a confused Roman got the plant mixed up with an evil-smelling cress, which presumably caused him to wrinkle up or "twist" his nose in distaste.

But don't let that discourage you from using nasturtiums—flower, leaf, and stem—in salads or as a garnish.

Shred the blossoms and add them to cottage cheese. Prettier than chives, and tastier, too. (I always think cottage cheese needs all the help it can get in the glamour department.)

Break up the crisp, tangy stems and sprinkle them in a green salad or in potato salad or deviled eggs.

The leaves, too, have a spicy, refreshing flavor and are delicious when combined with lettuce.

The following recipe is from a *Cookery Book & Household Guide,* published in 1896.

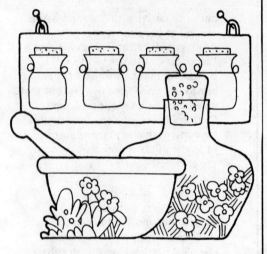

How to Prepare Pickled Nasturtiums
Ingredients: To each pint of vinegar: 1 oz. salt, 6 peppercorns, nasturtiums.

Gather the nasturtium pods [seeds] on a dry day and wipe them clean with a cloth; put them in a dry glass bottle, with the vinegar, salt, and peppercorns. If you cannot find enough ripe to fill a bottle, cork up what you have got until more are fit: they may be added from day to day. Bung up the bottle and seal or resin the top. They will be fit for use in 10 or 12 months; and the best way is to make them one season for the next.

Petunia
You just can't beat petunias for masses of color and abundance of bloom from spring on into the fall. Use the single varieties (grandifloras) for bedding and edging. The double and giant ruffled varieties are better suited to containers, because the large blooms are fragile.

Colors include red, white, purple, yellow, blue, pink, cream, purple-and-white striped, red-and-white striped. Go ahead, plant a rainbow!

Tips to Make You Tops with Petunias
1. Be sure to give them a location where they will have at least a half day of sun, preferably more, in the coastal and inner coastal areas. Inland they like partial shade.
2. They do best in a soil that is on the sandy side, not too rich and loamy.
3. These are tender annuals, so start the seed indoors and transplant when nights are staying above 55 degrees. For quick color, start with the bedding plants.

(See **The Art of Starting from Seeds and Bedding Plants,** *January.*)

4. Space the plants 6 to 8 inches apart, depending on the effect you are striving for—whether an edging (use the dwarf plants for this) or a colorful bed.
5. Water at the ground level rather than overhead. (One of the few problems petunias encounter is watermold fungus, encouraged by such practices as late afternoon or evening watering and over-head watering. (See **The Art of Watering,** *May.*)
6. Don't overfeed. An occasional snack such as a low-nitrogen fertilizer is best, but too much nitrogen produces foliage at the expense of bloom.
7. Keep faded flowers picked, and pinch back stem ends to make the plants more compact and to increase bloom. (See **The Art of Pinching Back,** *April.*)

FOUR BEAUTY SPOTS FOR MARCH PLANTING

You can be your own landscape architect! Here are four suggested combinations of plants with similar sun, shade, soil, and moisture needs. These small adventures in color and form are designed to beautify problem areas or to brighten dull sections of the garden. Start with these, then try working out your own designs.

NAME	HEIGHT (INCHES) & SUGGESTED COLORS	SUN/SHADE	SOIL
Seeds or Bedding Plants:			
For a "Glorious Fourth" Beauty Spot, try this red, white, and blue combination:			
Forget-me-not	8, blue	Sun	Average
Petunias	6-12, white	Sun	Average
Verbena	6-12, red	Sun	Average
Seeds:			
Ageratum, Dwarf	6, blue	Sun	Average
Marigold, Dwarf	6, yellow, gold	Sun	Average
In a circular bed, marigolds in center, ringed with ageratum; in borders, alternate.			
Candytuft (annual)	8-10, lavender, pink, white rose	Sun	Well drained
Marigold, Dwarf	6, yellow	Sun	Average
Pansy	8-10, mixed	Sun	Well drained
This makes a spectacular grouping in a circular or triangular bed, with the candytuft as the central plant, edged with marigolds and/or pansies. (Mulch the pansies with compost.) This is the annual candytuft, which gives a solid spread of color.			
Bedding Plants:			
Campanula (Dalmatian Bellflower)	4-6, blue	Sun, partial shade	Well drained
Shasta Daisy	24, white	Sun, partial shade	Well drained

OTHER PLANTABLES FOR MARCH

Here are additional plants that may be started this month. The planting information will be found in the chapters indicated below by month. Unless otherwise shown, reference is to "Let's Get Growing" section.

SEEDS

Ageratum	*April;* also *March* "Beauty Spots"
Candytuft, annual	*April;* also *September* "Beauty Spots"
Gaillardia	*January;* also *July* "Beauty Spots"
Hollyhock	*February*
Marigold	*April;* also *March* and *June* "Beauty Spots"
Portulaca	*August*
Shasta Daisy	*May, August*
Sunflower	*April*
Sweet Alyssum	*August, November*
Verbena	*January;* also *March* "Beauty Spots"
Vinca Rosea	*May*

BEDDING PLANTS

Ageratum	*April;* also *March* "Beauty Spots"
Aster	*July*
Begonia	*June, May*
Campanula	*July, August*
Candytuft perennial	*August, November*
Carnation	*January*
Coral Bells	*July; June* "Beauty Spots"
Delphinium	*February, April, July*
Gaillardia	*January;* also *July* "Beauty Spots"
Gazania	*August*
Gloriosa Daisy	*June*
Marigold	*April;* also *March* and *June* "Beauty Spots"
Phlox	*May*
Portulaca	*August*
Salvia	*May* "Beauty Spots"
Scabiosa (Pincushion Flower)	*July* "Beauty Spots"
Verbena	*January;* also *March* "Beauty Spots"
Vinca Rosea	*May*

BULBS

Begonia, Tuberous	*June, May*
Dahlia	*April*
Gladiola	*February, May, November*

PLANT DIVISIONS OR GALLON CANS

Agapanthus (Lily of the Nile)	*June*
Daylily	*May, August, October*
Delphinium	*February*
Fuchsia	*April, March*
Geum	*July*
Verbena	*January;* also *March* "Beauty Spots"

April

Plant of the Month: Sunflower. It dates back to the Inca civilization, where it was venerated as a symbol of the sun god. Dramatic in size and height, it's way up there as an edible plant, too—the roasted seeds are delicious.

April

The Hurry-Up-and-Plant Month—Except for the Heat Lovers

April's anger is swift to fall,
April's wonder is worth it all.
—Sir Henry Newbolt

The Romans knew what they were about when they named April—it means "to open." And there's a lot of that going on in Southern California gardens this time of year.

The door is open now for many of the summer-blooming annuals. It's a great time to get bedding plants of perennials settled in their new homes, too. Roses are on the verge of their long blooming season, which will continue, with brief pauses, right into December. The danger of even a late frost is past now, and we can sow almost any seed where we want it to stay, with few exceptions.

But the verse above carries a small warning. April is a capricious month, given to whims of wind and rain and cloudy weather. Southern California springs can be chilly affairs. We are sure to get periods of heavy overcast for the next two months, and sometimes well into June. So hold off planting heat-loving annuals this month. Zinnias, for example, will just sit there and sulk. You're wise to wait until the ground has warmed up, in May or even as late as June.

While you're waiting for the weather to stop fooling around, get the beds and borders ready by adding steer manure, compost, balanced fertilizers. Use about a half pound of steer manure to a square foot of soil. Some bone meal worked into the soil gives good nourishment for the roots of the things you will set out. There's an advantage to doing these things a couple of weeks in advance. It gives the nutrients time to get worked into the soil, and in the case of steer manure, it eliminates any danger of burning tender roots.

DO IT NOW

Azaleas and Camellias

Azaleas should be shaped now. Cut or break off (they snap off easily, so you need not even bother with pruning shears) just enough of the ends of the branches to achieve the natural, unmanicured look that is the azalea's native style. As little as 1 or 2 inches will be sufficient.

Camellias should be trimmed as soon as they finish blooming, before the new growth starts. Once those bright green new leaves are out, you can't prune without sacrificing the next season's bloom. Cut or break off at a point close to a live leaf bud, or axil. (*Axil:* Conversational Gardenese for that point where the branch diverges from the stem to which it is attached.) Remove just enough to shape the plant or to keep it from interfering with adjoining plants.

Delphinium

If they were set out in February, they will need a feeding of fish fertilizer now. (See **The Art of Fertilizing,** *March.*) There should be no confusion as to amounts to "feed" plants. Just moisten the soil as you would if you were using only water. In using any fertilizer, always water before and after.

Check the stakes for delphiniums. If they were set in place at time of planting, winds or heavy rains may have left them a little wobbly. If you did not stake earlier, better do it now; we may get some blustery weather this month. Be sure to place the stake at least 6 inches from the stem to avoid injuring the roots.

THE ART OF STAKING

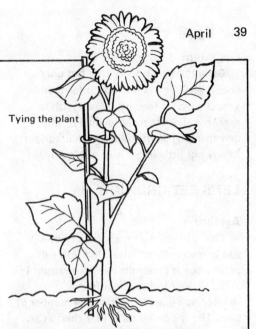
Tying the plant

Why Stake? To support tall or heavy-headed plants. To give protection against strong winds or heavy rains. To give added foundation support to shallow-rooted plants.

What to Use. For tall plants such as sunflowers, dahlias, poinsettias, use 6- or 8-foot-long 1-by-1-inch redwood. For smaller plants, such as marigolds (the 3-to-4-foot African variety) and bushy plants such as Shasta daisies and chrysanthemums, use the slim bamboo stakes—the 2-, 3-, or 4-foot heights. When in place, the stake should be approximately three-fourths of the plant's height. This makes it less conspicuous, and the weight or pull of the plant is not likely to sway the stake.

How to Stake. Ideally, staking should be done at the time of planting. (See "Dahlias," below.) In this way, there is no danger of injuring the roots as there is if the stake is pushed down into the ground after the roots are established. When staking after the plant is growing, set the stake at least 6 inches from the crown (center) of the plant. The smaller, bushy plants can be staked or supported when the need arises, since there is less hazard to the roots when the narrow bamboo stakes are used.

Tying the Plant. The tie that binds can be the tie that cuts or breaks. Never tie plant and stake tightly together. Use gardener's twine (raffia), cord, or "twist-ties." The double-loop method is best for the tall plants. Tie the cord around the stake, then bring the ends around the plant's stalk, and tie. This gives strong support, but prevents rubbing or cutting.

Lower-growing plants may be supported individually with the slim bamboo stakes, using the same method. Bushy plants such as chrysanthemums or Shasta daisies need a little different treatment. Set four bamboo stakes of the appropriate height around the plant, about 8 inches from the base, and circle with cord or other material.

Remember: Your stakes can be reused. Take them up when the need is past, clean off any soil, and store them.

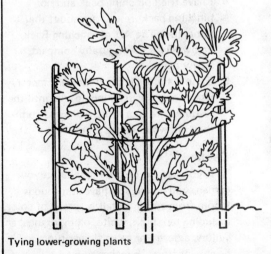
Tying lower-growing plants

Geranium

Geraniums get hungry too, but only once a year. This is the month for their annual nitrogen feeding. Organic fish is excellent. Too-frequent feeding of this undemanding plant will result in luxuriant foliage but little in the way of bloom.

LET'S GET GROWING

Ageratum

This distinctive annual of many uses is also known as floss flower, but you will usually buy it under the name ageratum. It is virtually pest- and problem-free, long-blooming, and effective in a number of ways. Use the dwarf form (6 inches) as an edging or as a solid bed of blue, edged with yellow violas. Mix it in with other plants in its taller form (12 inches or more). The pink and white varieties are not as common (and not as effective, in my opinion) as the blue.

Tips to Make You Tops with Ageratum
1. Start the seed now in flats, or set out the bedding plants. (See **The Art of Starting from Seeds and Bedding Plants,** *January.*) It needs full sun in coastal and inner coastal gardens, partial shade in the hot interiors.
2. Average soil is all it needs, but if your soil is on the heavy side, add compost or other organic matter to lighten it and to improve the water-holding properties.
3. Ageratum wants to be well-watered throughout the summer and will reward you by blooming into October.
4. Give it a feeding of a low-nitrogen fertilizer once a month. (See **The Art of Fertilizing,** *March.*) Use a liquid fish fertilizer, pouring enough around each plant to moisten the soil (about one-half cup). Be sure to water before and after to dilute the fertilizer, in case it is too strong, and to carry it down to the root zone.

Candytuft, Annual

A solid bed of candytuft ringed with pansies is a traffic-stopper. This is the annual variety of Iberis, also called *globe candytuft.* The dwarf variety gets up to 8 inches, the taller to around 12—but it's an easy-to-grow, no-problem plant. The close-growing clusters of pink, white, rose, and lavender blossoms spread a carpet of bloom from May to mid-July. It doesn't like the hot weather, so when the temperature ranges in the 90s, candytuft will taper off.

Tips to Make You Tops with Candytuft
1. Sow seeds where you want them to grow, since transplanting slows them down a bit.
2. They need a good water supply, so be sure the soil is light and well drained. It doesn't need to be especially rich or loamy. Keep the seeds moist until germination (about two weeks—longer, if the weather is chilly).
3. When seedlings are about 2 inches high, thin to 4 inches apart. Don't toss out the ones you remove in thinning, transplant them; they will develop a little more slowly but be just as husky in the long run.
4. I have tried pinching back and not pinching back; results are about the same. (See **The Art of Pinching Back,** below.) This is a naturally compact, bushy plant.
5. Good watering is the important factor. Use a fogger or seedling nozzle until the seedlings are 3 or 4 inches high. From then on, water at the base.

Dahlia

If you had nothing but dahlias in your garden, you would still have continuous bloom from spring to fall; a spread of color, including red, pink, white, plum, orange, and yellow; a dozen or more flower types in heights of from 15 inches to 5 feet.

THE ART OF PINCHING BACK

What. Pinching back, an important aspect of gardening, is the practice of removing the tip of a seedling to promote growth.

Why. It redirects the plant's energy or growth; little buds at the axils shoot out to become branches. Result: a bushy plant with lots of bloom instead of a tall, spindly one with sparse bloom.

How. With thumb and forefinger, gently pinch off the tip of the stem.

When. Wait until the seedlings have at least three sets of leaves. If they have been started in flats and then transplanted, wait three or four days, until they get over the shock of transplanting.

Some plants that respond to pinching back are:

Ageratum	Painted Tongue
Calendula	Petunia
Chrysanthemum	Phlox
Dahlia	Schizanthus
Dianthus	Snapdragon
Dusty Miller	Sweet Pea
Geranium	Verbena
Nemesia	Zinnia

Many plants with a naturally branching, sprawling, or tall growth pattern should be left to follow their natural bent. For example: hollyhocks, nasturtiums, poppies, sunflowers, and a long list of *et ceteras.*

Others should be pinched back at the tip of the main stem after the "true" leaves appear and, in addition, should have a methodical pinching back of the tips of the side branches or "laterals" as they develop. Dahlias, chrysanthemums, and geraniums are in this category. (See *May,* "Do It Now," for instructions on pinching back chrysanthemums.)

They demand some special consideration, since they must be "lifted" (taken out of the ground and stored) in the fall, separated (propagated by cutting the tubers from the parent stem), replanted in the spring, and staked in order to support the heavy flower heads. They're worth every bit of it!

Tips to Make You Tops with Dahlias

1. Select a sunny location (a minimum of six hours of sun) but in the interior valleys protect them from the midday sun.
2. Good drainage is essential. If your soil is clayey or heavy, work in compost or peat moss and sand to lighten it. If you add steer manure, delay planting for a week or so to avoid burning the tubers. Bone meal (1 pound worked into a planting area of 20 square feet) gets the tubers off to a good start, also.
3. Work the soil to a depth of 1 foot, then fill in to within 6 inches of the surface.
4. Set the stake in, then place the tuber about 1 inch from it. The tuber must have the eye up. Cover it with 3 inches of soil.

5. Water at the time of planting, about a pint per tuber; then withhold water until the first shoots appear.
6. Gradually fill in with the remaining soil as the shoots get taller; keep the soil moist. How often, will depend on the temperature and on the soil. Every other day will probably suffice.
7. Pinch off the top of the center stalk when the plant has three sets of leaves.
8. When the leaves are fully developed, feed with a low-nitrogen fertilizer (2-10-10). (See **The Art of Fertilizing,** *March.*) Until this time, the tubers contain sufficient nourishment for the plant.
9. Secure stems to the stakes when the plant reaches a height of 3 feet. Tie loosely, just enough to steady and support the stem, at two or three points. (See **The Art of Staking**, above.)
10. As the plants mature and begin to set buds, begin deep-watering. This means letting the hose run slowly at the base of the plant until the soil is wet to an approximate depth of 10 or 12 inches. Once a week should be sufficient for deep-watering. (See **The Art of Watering,** *May.*) On hot days give the plants a gentle overhead spray at mid-morning, but not if temperature is in the 90s or higher.

You can also start your dahlia garden with the bedding plants, Unwins. These are small singles and doubles grown from seed. They form their own tubers, so you get a lasting bonus. These don't need any staking, but sun, soil, and water needs are the same as above. Lift and store in the fall. (See "Dahlia," *November.*)

Fuchsia

There is probably no other plant of comparable beauty that requires so little special care, but that little is important. They need the coastal and inner coastal climates for the most satisfying results. Their preference is for coolness, shade, and a humid atmosphere. In gardens of the hot interior valleys they require overhead lath protection, screening from the dry winds, and careful attention to their moisture needs.

Tips to Make You Tops with Fuchsias
1. Give them a shady, sheltered location with moist, loamy, well-drained soil.
2. Don't fertilize new young plants, but let the tender roots mature at their own pace. Compost or leaf mold will provide the necessary nutrients until the plant is well established, showing steady growth. Then feed with organic fish fertilizer every other week, from March to October. (See **The Art of Fertilizing,** *March.*)
3. Water them overhead in hot weather to create the humid atmosphere they need, and deep-water every other day in the summer months.
4. Don't neglect keeping them adequately watered in the dormant period (October to February).
5. Mulch in the summer months. (See **The Art of Mulching,** *February.*)
6. Cut back lightly after the bloom period to promote another round of bloom—about half the amount done in spring. (See *March,* "Do It Now.")
7. Water the underside of the leaves at least once a week, to discourage spider mites and aphids.

8. Control infestations of white fly or leafhoppers with rotenone or pyrethrum. Hand-pick any leaf worms. (See **The Art of Pest Control**, *March.*)
9. When buying fuchsias, avoid the large plant in the small pot; it usually means the roots are pot-bound, and the plant starts out at a disadvantage in your garden. Be sure to specify whether you want to use the plant in a hanging basket or not; there are both upright and trailing varieties.
10. If you live in the hot, dry areas, ask the nursery about heat-resistant varieties.

Geranium

Plant geraniums any time of the year in Southern California. Fast-growing and easy to propagate from cuttings, they give an incredible range of color and variety and ask little in the way of care.

There was a time when they were so common in Southern California, growing wild along the roadsides and in vacant lots, that they were underrated by most of us. The Martha Washingtons have always been prestigious, however. Sometimes called "poor man's azalea," they are the exotics of the geranium family.

In May of each year, the Southwest Branch of the International Geranium Society holds its annual Geranium and Pelargonium Show in Los Angeles. In addition to the displays, many plants are for sale. This is a great way to discover the multitudinous varieties of this popular plant. (Watch your local newspaper for date and place of the show.)

The *scents-ible ones* are fun to collect: apple, apricot, cinnamon, lemon, lime, nutmeg, peppermint, and rose, each with appropriately scented foliage. Blossoms of the scented geraniums are negligible; the treasure lies in the leaves. Keep them

trimmed back, and use the trimmings to start cuttings.

Zonals are distinguished by the markings or color zones on the leaves. They are profuse bloomers, but it is the color combinations—whites and greens, golds and bronzes, in a variety of patterns on the foliage—that make them attractive.

Ivy geraniums are climbers. The ivy-shaped leaves and abundant flowers, in white, pink, or red, make them attractive in hanging baskets, as groundcovers, or climbing over walls or fences.

The *Martha Washington,* also called Lady Washington, or Regal, is the glamour girl of the geranium family and is usually the one we think of as pelargonium. Which opens up that perennial puzzle: When is a geranium not a geranium but a pelargonium? And the answer is never, because they belong to the same family. *Geranium* is the name most generally used, so let's stick with that.

The Martha Washington has such a variety of colors and color combinations that it would be hard to cover them all. They range from pale pink to maroon and white. The Martha Washington is just as easy to grow and to propagate as any other geranium, happy in a pot or in the ground.

Tips to Make You Tops with Geraniums
1. Give them a sunny location, although the Martha Washington and the zonals will do well in partial shade.
2. Good drainage is the primary concern, so add organic matter (such as compost, leaf mold, or peat moss) to the soil if it is on the clayey side. But geraniums definitely do not need a rich, loamy soil.
3. Avoid overfeeding. Too much nitrogen, especially, will produce luxuriant foliage but little bloom.
4. Never water geraniums overhead, except early in the day (before 10:00 a.m.) so that they will dry off completely before

EAT YOUR PLANT AND HAVE IT TOO: GERANIUM TEA

Tea drinkers can add a gourmet touch to that beverage by dropping a scrap of rose geranium leaf into the pot as the hot water is added. How big a scrap depends on your taste, as well as on the amount of tea being brewed.

The foliage of the peppermint geranium is tasty, also—more aromatic than the delicate flavor of rose geranium.

Peppermint geranium tea is an intensely refreshing, aromatic beverage, one of those grandmotherly potions from the past. Try it when you have a heavy cold.

To Prepare Peppermint Geranium Tea

Wash and shred five or six freshly picked leaves from which the stems have been removed. Place in a teapot and pour two cups of boiling water over the leaves. Cover and let it steep for several hours. Later strain and reheat it.

---

evening. The best procedure is to water them at ground level.

5. Geraniums are drought-resistant. Allow them to dry out between waterings, but soak the soil thoroughly when you water.

6. The tender discipline of pinching back or pruning is quite important, since geraniums have a tendency to become straggly or "woody." This can be done at any time, and the prunings used to start new plants. (See **The Art of Propagation from Softwood Cuttings,** *March,* and **The Art of Pinching Back,** *April.*)

7. The few problems geraniums have are usually caused by wrong watering practices. Stem rot, in which the stems rot at the base, is a water-mold fungus disease that results from too frequent watering and from crowding of plants. Bacterial leaf spot, which manifests itself as small brown areas on the lower, older leaves, can be caused by overhead watering late in the day, and also by placing plants too close together, which creates a humid condition.

Marigold

Marigolds can be started now. Seeds are fast-germinating (three to six days), and you have an even faster start if you buy the bedding plants.

The marigold is more than just another pretty face around the garden. Wherever it is planted, it is believed to rid the soil of nematodes. These are tiny, threadlike pests that winter in the soil; they particularly like our mild Southern California winters and the loose, loamy soils we work so hard to achieve. (They have trouble moving around in heavy, clayey soils, where the particles are closely packed.)

Most nematode damage is to the roots of plants, and since marigold roots are presumed to give off a substance that is toxic to the nematodes, it makes good sense to plant this hearty and versatile flower.

The fact that snails would rather eat marigolds than any other plant in the garden can be an advantage or a disadvantage, depending on how you look at it. The snails that are happily munching your marigolds are not bothering with other plants in the vicinity to any great extent. However, in years of heavy snail infestations, an entire bed of marigolds can be demolished overnight, so it's smart to start the seeds in flats and wait until the seedlings are a sturdy 4 inches before transplanting to their permanent home.

The African marigold is bushy and tall—to 3 or 4 feet—with attractive foliage and 3- to 5-inch double blooms in yellow, gold, or orange. It will flower without pause, from late spring into November and will form a veritable hedge, if spaced 10 to 12 inches apart.

The dwarf marigold is a 6-inch-high duplicate of the tall; the French marigold is somewhere in between the African and the dwarf in height, but with a distinctive blossom combining petals of reddish mahogany with yellow or orange.

There really is gold in these flowers, not just in the name. For over fifty years, the W. Atlee Burpee Co. offered a prize of $10,000 to the first person to develop a white marigold. In 1975, Mrs. Alice Vonk of Sully, Iowa, produced the "great white hope" of the veteran seed company. No one has come up with a name for what is probably the most expensive flower ever produced (the Burpee Company spent a quarter of a million in research and testing). Here's my suggestion: call it *Mariwhite*.

Tips to Make You Tops with Marigolds

1. Plant the seeds every three weeks from now until July for a succession of bloom.
2. They are the least fussy of flowers, requiring not a rich soil, but a well-drained one, five or six hours of sun per day.
3. They are thirsty ones, especially the tall African variety. Water all varieties at the ground level; the stems are brittle and will sometimes bend just below the blossom if watered overhead. Soak them daily.
4. You won't find it necessary to feed marigolds, but it never hurts to give any plant a good start with well-worked soil to which a balanced fertilizer and perhaps some bone meal have been added. (See **The Art of Fertilizing,** *March.*) This is one of the most satisfactory flowers you

can grow. It's a good cut flower, if you don't mind the rather strong odor, and, with the exception of the aforementioned snails, virtually pest- and problem-free.

Incidentally, if you want to splurge a little, buy bedding plants of the Nugget (a foot high) and First Lady (around 18 inches). Because these superior grades are sterile (producing no seed), all of their energy is concentrated on flower production. They cost more than the common types, but are so prolific they are worth the difference.

Sunflower

Sunflowers are fun flowers. Ideally suited to our Southern California summers, this state flower of Kansas is much more than the country giant we tend to consider it. In fact, it has a background of nobility—the Incas of Peru venerated it as a symbol of their sun god.

The seeds are a valued source of an oil similar to olive oil. Roasted they make delicious snacking; rich, nourishing, tasty—and economical when you grow your own. Robert Shostek, in his *Lexicon of International Flowers and Plants* (Quadrangle, 1974), reports that sunflower seed husks can be used to make a beverage resembling coffee. Keep that in mind as coffee prices head higher than the sunflower plant!

Tips to Make You Tops with Sunflowers

1. Plant now for July or August bloom. There is a dwarf variety that grows to a mere 15 inches and gets its name, Cut-and-Come-Again, from its repeating pattern of blooming. However, the traditional sunflower, and the real achiever, is Helianthus Giganteus.

2. With a name like sunflower, you know it wants full sun—five or six hours a day.

3. Good drainage is vital, so work some organic material such as compost or peat moss into the soil. Dig to a depth of 12 to 18 inches. The height of the mature plant, plus the size and weight of foliage and blossoms (the flowers average a foot in diameter), make solid anchorage important.

EAT YOUR PLANT AND HAVE IT TOO: SUNFLOWER SEEDS

Let the flower heads go to seed. Protect from birds by slipping a plastic bag over each flower. Don't tie it on; let it hang loose. (You might like to leave one uncovered, if only for the fun of watching the birds dig out each seed as they cling to the face of the flower.) When the seeds begin to turn brown, cut the flower head off.

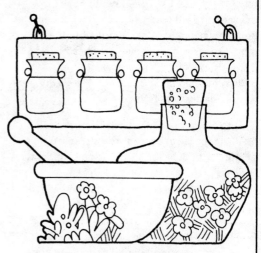

How to Prepare Seeds

Remove them from the flower head and place them in a saltwater solution: 1 teaspoon of salt to a quart of water. Leave them in the solution for half an hour. Then spread the seeds on a paper towel for 10 minutes to let excess moisture drain off.

Meanwhile, preheat the oven to 225 degrees. Spread the seeds on a cookie sheet or a sheet of aluminum foil. Place in the oven for 30 minutes. Then increase oven temperature to 350 degrees and roast for 15 minutes.

When cool, place in jars and cover tightly. Shelling or hulling is done as they are eaten.

The hulled seeds are delicious sautéed. Place them in a skillet, add 1 tablespoon of butter or margarine. Stir over low heat to brown evenly. Sprinkle with salt. Serve them hot or cold. To store, cool and place in jars as above.

If you are planting them primarily for the seeds, four or five plants should satisfy the nibbling needs of a family of four.

4. Set 8-foot redwood stakes in at time of soil preparation. (Redwood is not mandatory, but it's practical because it won't rot.)

5. Fill the hole to within an inch of the surface, and plant the seeds a half-inch deep, 18 to 24 inches apart.

6. As the seedlings grow, "earth up" (conversational Gardenese for heaping the soil around the stem) until the soil is mounded around the stem to about 6 inches above the soil surface. This will furnish additional support as the plant reaches its maximum height.

7. Water three or four times a week in hot weather, but not to the point of sogginess, which can weaken the plant at the surface level—remember, it is carrying a lot of weight.

If your aims are strictly decorative, use sunflowers in rows against a wall or as a living screen. They don't combine well with other plants. They are too overpowering in size and design. Also, the foliage reacts badly to crowding; it gets ragged and brown and generally unattractive.

FOUR BEAUTY SPOTS FOR APRIL PLANTING

You can be your own landscape architect! Here are four suggested combinations of plants with similar sun, shade, soil, and moisture needs. These small adventures in color and form are designed to beautify problem areas or to brighten dull sections of the garden. Start with these, then try working out your own designs.

NAME	HEIGHT (INCHES) & SUGGESTED COLORS	SUN/SHADE	SOIL
Seeds:			
Blue Marguerite	18, blue	Sun	Average
Hunnemannia	24, yellow	Sun	Average
Bedding Plants:			
Begonia Semperflorens (Snowbank)	6-8, white flowers, light green foliage	Shade, filtered sun	Light, well drained
Coleus	6-24, multihued foliage	Shade, filtered sun	Light, well drained
Bedding Plants:			
Blue Cupflower	6-12, blue	Sun, light shade	Well drained
Penstemon	24-36, white, pink	Sun, light shade	Well drained
Seeds:			
Cockscomb, Dwarf	6-12, red, orange	Sun	Average
Petunia, Dwarf	6, white	Sun	Average

OTHER PLANTABLES FOR APRIL

Here are additional plants that may be started this month. The planting information will be found in the chapters indicated below by month. Unless otherwise shown, reference is to "Let's Get Growing" section.

SEEDS

Alyssum, Saxatile	*November*	Portulaca	*August*
Anchusa	*May* "Beauty Spots"	Sweet Alyssum	*August, November*
Cockscomb	*July;* also *April* "Beauty Spots"	Verbena	*January;* also *March* "Beauty Spots"
Cosmos	*May* "Beauty Spots"	Vinca Rosea	*May*
Nasturtium	*March;* also *June* "Beauty Spots"		

BEDDING PLANTS

Alyssum, Saxatile	*November*	Gloriosa Daisy	*June*
Aster	*July*	Hollyhock	*February*
Begonia	*June, May*	Marguerite	*March;* also *July* "Beauty Spots"
Blue Cupflower	*April* "Beauty Spots"	Penstemon	*January;* also *April* "Beauty Spots"
Campanula	*July, August;* also *March* "Beauty Spots"	Petunia	*March*
Carnation	*January*	Phlox	*May*
Coleus	*March*	Portulaca	*August*
Columbine	*February* "Beauty Spots"	Rosea	*May*
Coral Bells	*July;* also *June* "Beauty Spots"	Salvia	*May* "Beauty Spots"
Delphinium	*February, April, July*	Scabiosa	*May;* also *July* "Beauty Spots"
Dianthus	*May* "Beauty Spots"	Sweet Alyssum	*August, November*
Forget-me-not	*March* "Beauty Spots"	Verbena	*January;* also *March* "Beauty Spots"
Gaillardia	*January*		
Gazania	*August*		
Geum	*July*		

BULBS

Begonia, Tuberous	*June, May*	Gladiola	*February, May, November*
Canna	*March, November*	Tuberose	*May* "white garden"

PLANT DIVISIONS OR GALLON CANS

Columbine	*February* "Beauty Spots"	Fuchsia	*April, June, July*
Daylily	*May, August, October*	Marguerite	*March;* also *July* "Beauty Spots"
Delphinium	*February*		

May

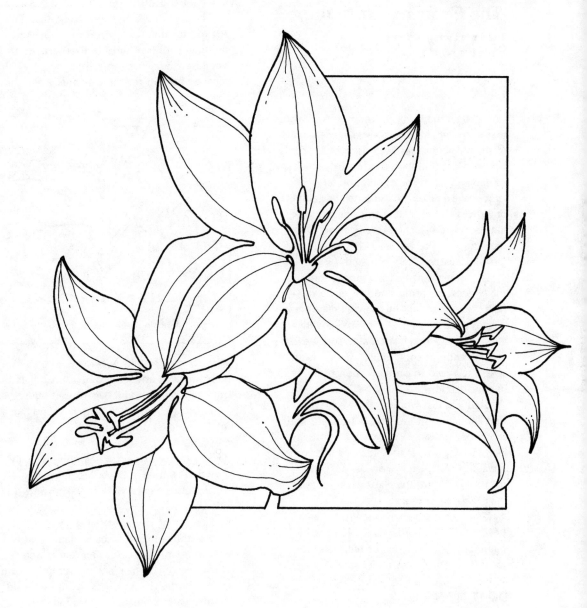

Plant of the Month: Daylily. It has just about everything a gardener could ask for: hundreds of varieties in beautiful colors; no pests, no problems. On top of all that, it's good to eat!

May

The Growing-est Month

**Feed the spring-bloomers,
plant the heat-lovers.**

We're on the brink of summer. And while that may seem hard to believe in the middle of the foggy, overcast weather we get at this time of year, Southern Californians—the gardening part of the population, at least—have a ready answer when newcomers or visitors complain that this doesn't look like "sunny California." We cock an eye at the slate-gray sky and say, "It's wonderful growing weather, isn't it?" And it is.

The Romans named the month for Maia, the goddess of spring, and it is really the high point of the spring growing season. We are transplanting a lot of the seedlings we've nursed along from March and April sowing, and this cool, moist weather is just what they need to get their roots established in new locations.

Seedlings just working their way up will find enough sun to suit them (we get *some* sunny days in May!), but they are not likely to dry out, as they may do later on if we don't keep an eye on them. (Once the roots dry out, the plant never recovers the old get-up-and-grow energy.)

May puts the *plan* into plant. It's a good time to redesign borders and beds and to figure out replacements for bulbs and the early-flowering annuals.

DO IT NOW

Azaleas and Camellias

These should have their second feeding the middle of the month. (See **The Art of** Fertilizing, *March.*) Be sure to water the granules of dry food in thoroughly.

Chrysanthemum

These should be pinched back. (See **The Art of Pinching Back**, *April.*) Remove the terminal (tip) leaf buds to divert growth to side branches. These, in turn, should be pinched back in the same manner when they

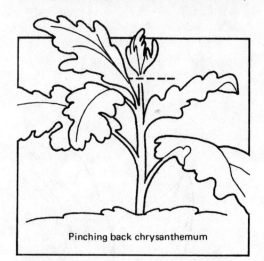

Pinching back chrysanthemum

grow to roughly 5 inches. Keep up the pinching back until August 1st. Stop then, because the plants will begin to set buds.

This matter of pinching may sound like a lot of fuss over nothing; but if chrysanthemums are left to their own devices they will run to long, thin, scraggly growth, resulting in fewer blooms and necessitating a great deal of staking and tying.

Exception: If you are training your chrysanthemum as a cascade plant—that is, with long, trailing, cascading stems—don't pinch back until the plant is a foot high, and then only the tip, and later the resulting side shoots, when they are 4 inches long.

Keep up an every-other-week feeding program with the chrysanthemums until buds are well enough along to show tinges of color.

As in most gardening procedures, you should adjust to the particular need. If your chrysanthemums have as many as five basal stems, you should do less pinching back—perhaps none at all—since this development assures a fairly bushy, substantial growth pattern.

Gerbera

A pleasant paradox of gardening is that you increase by dividing. May is the month to divide gerberas (Transvaal daisies).

If you have been overlooking this plant (fast becoming a Southern California specialty) as "just another daisy," go to a nursery and see what you've been dismissing: handsome blossoms, 4 or 5 inches across, with slightly curving petals in colors of yellow to orange, salmon pink to rose—rising on curving, leafless stems from gray-green foliage.

In coastal and inner coastal areas, gerberas will bloom, with varying abundance, from May to December. If you live in the San Fernando or San Gabriel valleys or in any of the hot inland sections, give them partial shade. Otherwise, they want full sun.

To divide, gently loosen the soil in a circle around the gerbera, using a spading fork, and pry up the plant. Carefully pull the

Dividing gerbera

clump apart and set the sections into prepared, watered holes. Ample room must be made for the roots, so the soil should be worked deeper and wider than the division that is to be set into it. Add compost or peat moss to improve the drainage, since this is one of the vital needs of the gerbera. How much to add depends on the soil; fill perhaps a quarter of the planting hole with compost or peat moss.

The division should be set a little high so that it is slightly above the surface of the soil, allowing for settling. Otherwise, soil washed over into the crown (the area between root and stem) will cause rot.

Mulch in extremely hot weather, with peat moss or compost, about an inch of mulch. (See **The Art of Mulching**, *February.*) Avoid watering directly on the crown area. Feed once a month with organic fish fertilizer. (See **The Art of Fertilizing,** *March.*)

Gladiola

May is that Glad time when the gladiolas planted in February are displaying their colorful spikes of bloom. Here's a tip for cutting them for bouquets: Gladiolas open from the bottom bud on up, so cut them when color is just beginning to show in those lower buds. Always leave at least three leaves because the corms (or bulbs) draw nourishment from the foliage after the bloom period is over. (See "Gladiolas," *February.*)

Poinsettia

Cut them back this month. (Make a slanting cut just above the third bud from the bottom of the stalk.) Feed now with a fertilizer high in nitrogen content. (See **The Art of Fertilizing,** *March.*)

Roses

Never give a sucker an even break where roses are concerned. The suckers

THE ART OF WATERING

There is a lot of speculation today about communicating with our plants—but if they ever get to the point where they can really express themselves, they'll probably have some pretty strong language on the subject of watering.

Watering is one of the most overlooked and underestimated of garden skills. Whether we err in the direction of too little, too much, or uneven distribution of water, the results can be disastrous. Overwatering is probably the most common offense. It can cause a lot of terrifying-sounding problems like damping-off, root rot, failure to set seed, edema, and some can't even spell.

Try this experiment: Take a pad and pencil and make the rounds of your garden, writing down the names of the various plants. Then look up the watering needs of each one. If your home has been occupied by a number of owners over the years, each has probably planted a few things, often on impulse, and so a plant that needs constant moisture may be growing next to one that needs to dry out between waterings. Some that need deep watering may be planted on a slope where the moisture runs off rapidly.

A survey such as this takes only a little time, but it is a valuable guide to future plantings and present care. Take the time and effort to find out the moisture requirements of your plants; not only the amounts of water, but the special techniques are important.

All of us have some watering habits that make life tough for our plants. Study the following performers in The Water Ballet, and see if you spot yourself in any of the roles:

The Sunbathers. They like to combine watering with getting a suntan, so they water in the hottest

(conversational Gardenese for secondary shoots) appear below the bud union (the bulge toward the bottom of the main stem). Remove them as soon as they appear. Use a knife or pruning shears.

Seedlings

Are you following through with the seedlings from all the seeds you planted earlier this spring? Don't let them stay too long in the containers, or the roots will get all wrapped up in each other, making it hard to separate the plants and adding to the shock of transplanting.

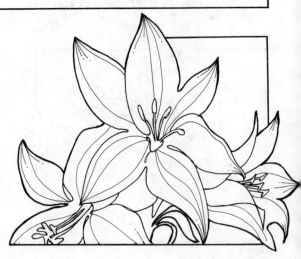

part of the day. While they're getting bronzed, their plants are getting sunburn, mildew, and various other problems. And much of the water is lost through evaporation.

The Sprinklers. They water everything lightly. A little bit here, a little bit there. "There! That's done!" they say. What's done is the damage. That small amount of water is just going to bake dry when the sun hits it, putting a crust on the soil surface. But worst of all, the roots have to come up to the surface for water under these conditions; and after a while they just hang around up there all the time, and eventually the plant dies of undernourishment.

The Waders. They like to pour it on! When they get through puddling around, it's Swan Lake in the garden, and the plants are going down for the third time. (Keep in mind that plants can drown if too much water stands in poorly drained soil.)

The Scooters. They like to use the hard spray called a sweeper nozzle; it's modeled along the lines of a fire hose nozzle. They spend most of their time scooting leaves off the lawn. But they don't stop there—the jet stream goes on over into the borders, and whoosh! go all the nice mulch and top soil.

The Owls. They like to fool around out there after dark. They're wearing sweaters, but the plants are standing there in their bare leaves. A great way to encourage fungus diseases, since the foliage stays wet all night.

The Fountains. They water everything overhead. They figure they're washing the dust off the foliage, and maybe even a few bugs (though the smart ones are hiding on the underside of the leaves). They think they're giving their plants tender, loving care, but they're also giving them lots of problems such as mildew and other fungus diseases. Yes, some plants thrive on overhead sprinkling—ferns, begonias, fuchsias, the humidity lovers—but even with them, overhead watering is not a substitute for gentle watering at soil level.

Did you recognize yourself among these performers? If so, better change your ways, or it's curtains for the garden!

LET'S GET GROWING

Daylily

The scientific or botanical name for daylily is Hemerocallis, which means "beautiful for a day," and this plant lives up to its name. Even so, don't let that phrase, "for a day," steer you away from it. Each stalk bears a minimum of five buds, opening at the rate of one a day. Because there are so many varieties—in the hundreds—it's fun to plant a number of the daylilies at intervals of several weeks, to ensure a progression of bloom over a large part of the year.

Daylilies are remarkably hardy, free from fungus diseases, and they don't attract insect pests. They are so problem-free and easy to grow that in many parts of the eastern United States they are "escapes," growing wild along the roadsides and in meadows as happily as in gardens. (*Escape* is conversational Gardenese for a plant that runs wild and maintains itself without cultivation.)

These flowers can be planted at any time of the year in many parts of Southern California, but certain varieties do better in specific areas. In the San Fernando Valley it

LIGHT UP THE NIGHT WITH A GARDEN OF WHITE

Planned for blooming in the hot months ahead, white flowers give an effect of cool serenity, seeming almost to glow in the darkness, shining through as colors never can. The white garden is not a new idea, but in California, where color is so abundant, the all-white planting tends to be overlooked.

Plant the white garden where it can be enjoyed from the vantage point of pool or patio area. A dark background of hedge or shrubbery is ideal.

What to plant? Try these for sighs:

Agapanthus, White (Lily-of-the-Nile)

A good bet for the white garden, it can be planted any time of the year. (See *June.*)

Begonia, Tuberous

This will add glamour to the white garden, but it is a little more demanding than others in the group. If you live in the hot interior valleys, the Bertini hybrids will be best for your garden. (See "Tuberous Begonias," *June.*)

Begonia, White Fibrous

This perennial makes a lovely edging, the blossoms showing up sharp and clear against the glossy foliage. Begonias are available as bedding plants now, or can be easily started from cuttings or divisions, if you have friends who will give you some.

Ground Rules. The red-leafed varieties adapt well to a sunny location; the green-leafed need some shade, inland. Give them loamy, well-drained soil and plenty of water. Mulch them, in the hot, inland areas.

Candytuft, Perennial

This is the ideal edging plant to "light the way" along the garden path at night in the white garden. One of the glowingest white plants around. (See **The Art of Bulb Covers,** *November,* for planting instructions.) Use the bedding plants, or start from cuttings of those you may have.

Daisy, Shasta

So right and so white, with their yellow centers accentuating the whiteness of the petals, they are available now in gallon cans at the nurseries. The double-petaled (duplex) Majestic is effective in the white garden, but there are many varieties and forms—singles, doubles, semidoubles; crested, frilled, and fringed; flowers from 2 to 7 inches in diameter; heights from the 8-inch Thumbelina to the 3½-foot Edgebrook Giant.

Note for flower arrangements: The flower heads will absorb color. Add food coloring to the water for the cut flowers, if you like to tamper with Nature's perfection.

Ground Rules. Give Shasta daisies a fairly rich soil and regular, thorough watering. The taller varieties will need supporting. They prefer full sun, but will grow in partial shade. They are relatively problem- and pest-free, but snails love them.

Few of the name varieties will reproduce from seed, because Shastas have been so hybridized, but the Roggeli strain (singles) will. But why bother? They are so easily propagated by division. (Divide them every two years.)

Gladiola

Gladiolas are classic additions to the white garden and can still be planted, until the end of June. White varieties include Arctic Snow, Mother Fischer, and Florence Nightingale. (See "Gladiolas," *February.*)

Phlox, Annual

The long hot summer is just what this Texas native likes. Seeds are available in separate colors, including white. Phloxes are particularly effective in the white garden at night because of the mounding flower form, which creates a solid swath of white. Plant the tall variety (1 to 2 feet) in the middle section, the dwarf (6 to 12 inches) at the front.

Ground Rules. Sow seeds outdoors now, and thin to 6 inches apart. (See **The Art of Starting from Seeds and Bedding Plants,** *January.*) They want well-drained soil; they like sun but will grow in partial shade. Water them regularly. When they begin to look bloomed out, late in the summer, cut them back to about 2 inches and they will give another round of bloom.

Tuberose

Waxen white blossoms on 2- or 3-foot stems add not only beauty but fragrance as well to the white garden. The variety called The Pearl is a large double flower, but there is a dwarf form that stays around 15 inches high. Spot them here and there in the garden, in groups of two or three. The fragrance is rather heavy and, as with many of the "scents-ible" ones, it is better to plant in small groups.

Ground Rules. This is a heat, sun, and moisture lover. Soil should be loose-textured and enriched with compost or peat moss to ensure good drainage. The tubers should show a touch of green at the stem end. Set them an inch deep, 6 inches apart, leaving the soil loose, not pressed down over them.

There is a knack to watering tuberoses in the early stages. Moisten well at time of planting, then withhold water *until shoots appear.* From then on, water regularly, the amount depending on weather and temperature. Moist-but-not-soggy is a good rule.

Whether or not to "lift" them in the fall (conversational Gardenese for digging and storing in a warm, dry place) will depend on how well-drained the soil is. If it is on the heavy side, the tubers may rot during the wet winter weather. But many people leave them in the ground and get several years of bloom.

Vinca Rosea
(Madagascar Periwinkle)

Get the bedding plants now for quick bloom. The white vinca is lovely contrasted with its own foliage, and does best in hot weather. It's a perennial, but you may want to keep renewing it from cuttings, as it gets leggy after a season or two.

Ground Rules. Give it average soil but plenty of water. It's practically failure-proof and will bloom well into the fall.

Plan additions to the white garden each season. The plants suggested here are just enough to get you started on a fascinating aspect of gardening.

EAT YOUR PLANT AND HAVE IT TOO: DAYLILIES

All that beauty—and edible, too! The blossoms are delicious when cooked as fritters. Wash them gently, dry on paper towels, dip in pancake batter, and deep fry.

The tubers, which look a little like peanuts and are borne in clusters on the roots, are delicious boiled in salted water or fried in butter.

Any store that stocks Oriental foods will have dried daylilies. They are used in many Chinese dishes, including soups and salads, and have been considered delicacies as far back as the T'ang Dynasty.

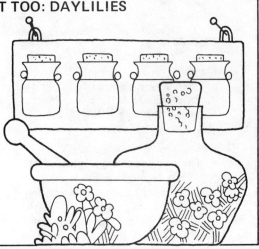

is possible to have almost year-round bloom, and there is no area of Southern California where they are not grown. Your local nursery can advise you as to the best varieties for your area.

Daylilies range in height from 1 to 5 feet, with an infinite variety of color in many shadings of yellow, gold, orange, salmon, cream, wine red, and a few bicolors. There is even that rarity, a green flower.

Tips to Make You Tops with Daylilies

1. Most daylilies need full sun, although some varieties must have partial shade in the afternoon.
2. Prepare the soil carefully with amendments of compost, peat moss, and sand, to guarantee good drainage. Planting holes should be worked to a depth of 12 inches, and a width of about 18 inches.
3. When the soil has settled after planting is done, the crown of the plant (that area between roots and stem) should be about an inch above the soil surface, so make allowances for this when you place the plant. Spread the roots slightly.
4. It will be in leaf at this time of year. Cut it back to about 5 inches. Water immediately after planting.
5. A week later, feed with organic fish fertilizer. (See **The Art of Fertilizing,** *March.*) From then on it will need only a once-a-year feeding with a low-nitrogen fertilizer.
6. Daylilies should be deep-watered once a week in dry weather, oftener in extreme temperatures. (See **The Art of Watering,** above.) This plant is an exception to the "water early in the day" rule. It is not subject to fungus diseases, so that hazard does not have to be considered in the matter of watering. Water it late in the afternoon or in the evening, since less moisture is lost through evaporation at that time.
7. Mulch with compost or peat moss before the hot weather arrives. If you use peat moss, be sure to keep it moist; otherwise it will form a crust and water will run off. (See **The Art of Mulching,** *February.*)
8. Keep the dead foliage clipped off.
9. Flower stems should be cut off as soon as the blossoms fade, in order to prevent formation of seed pods.

FOUR BEAUTY SPOTS FOR MAY PLANTING

You can be your own landscape architect! Here are four suggested combinations of plants with similar sun, shade, soil, and moisture needs. These small adventures in the use of color and form are designed to beautify problem areas or to brighten dull sections of the garden. Start with these, then try working out your own designs.

NAME	HEIGHT (INCHES) & SUGGESTED COLORS	SUN/SHADE	SOIL
Bedding Plants:			
Anchusa	18, blue	Sun	Average
Dianthus	16, red, rose, pink, white	Sun	Average
Seeds:			
Cosmos	36-48, white, pink, red	Sun, part shade	Average
Larkspur	36-48, blue, pink, white	Sun, part shade	Average
Bedding Plants:			
Dusty Miller	10-12, grayish white foliage	Sun	Average
Salvia	6-12, red	Sun	Average
Bedding Plants:			
Coreopsis	12-36, gold, orange, mahogany	Sun	Any
Scabiosa	18-30, pink, rose, blue, salmon, white	Sun	Fertile, well drained

OTHER PLANTABLES FOR MAY

Here are additional plants that may be started this month. The planting information will be found in the chapters indicated below by month. Unless otherwise shown, reference is to "Let's Get Growing" section.

SEEDS

Alyssum Saxatile	*November*	Nasturtium	*March;* also *June* "Beauty Spots"
Gaillardia	*January;* also *July* "Beauty Spots"	Portulaca	*August*
Marigold	*April;* also *March* "Beauty Spots"	Sunflower	*April*
		Sweet Alyssum	*August, November*
Mexican Fire Bush (Kochia)	*July*	Verbena	*January;* also *March* "Beauty Spots"
Moonflower	*July*	Zinnia	*June*

BEDDING PLANTS

Ageratum	*April;* also *March* "Beauty Spots"	Delphinium	*February, April, July*
		Forget-me-not	*March* "Beauty Spots"
Alyssum Saxatile	*November*	Gazania	*August*
Aster	*July*	Geranium	*April*
Campanula	*July, August;* also *March* "Beauty Spots"	Petunia	*March;* also *April* "Beauty Spots"
Candytuft, perennial	*April;* also *March* and *September* "Beauty Spots"	Portulaca	*August*
		Sweet Alyssum	*August, November*
Carnation	*January*	Zinnia	*June;* also *July* and *August* "Beauty Spots"
Chrysanthemum	*March, May, July*		
Coleus	*March*		
Coral Bell	*July, September;* also *June* "Beauty Spots"		

BULBS

Dahlia	*April, June, July, November*	Gladiola	*February, November*

PLANT DIVISIONS OR POTS

		Marguerite	*March;* also *July* "Beauty Spots"
Delphinium	*February*		
Dianthus	*May* "Beauty Spots"	Verbena	*January;* also *March* "Beauty Spots"
Geranium	*April*		

June

Plant of the Month: Zinnia. The hotter the weather, the more the zinnia flourishes; it's still around in the fall, when many of the other flowers have bowed out because of the heat. And what a color range! It's a long-lasting cut flower for summer bouquets, too.

June

The Take-It-Easy Month

**Last call for summer annuals,
first call for fall bloomers.**

June is named for Juno, the Roman deity of women and marriage—appropriately enough, since this is the month traditionally associated with brides. But legend says also that the name comes from the Latin, meaning "to join." And that's meaningful not only to those being joined in matrimony, but to gardening enthusiasts as well—it's the month when we link up with summer.

The longest day of the year falls on June 21 or 22, the time of the summer solstice, and summer officially begins then. Day length is a vital factor in plant growth, and as days begin to grow shorter after the summer solstice, so does our list of "plantables" for summer bloom.

It's a bit late for those summer-blooming annuals you didn't get around to earlier, so start them from bedding plants now; the hot days will slow seedlings down too much. So what? Sow heat-lovers! Celosia, zinnia, vinca rosea, and the ever-obliging, plant-any-month-of-the-year sweet alyssum.

Start some perennials from seed, transfer the seedlings to a special section of the garden, and then transplant at leisure in the fall, to enjoy next spring and summer, and many years after that.

DO IT NOW

African Daisy, Trailing
Trim off old, shaggy growth to encourage more bloom.

Azaleas and Camellias
If azaleas are looking dejected and down-in-the-leaf, they may be in need of some quick energy. Aluminum sulphate is quickly soluble, and gets to work at once, to remedy an acid-poor condition. Sprinkle it on the soil and water it in. Two heaping tablespoons will be sufficient for plants around 2 or 3 feet in height; double the amount for substantially larger plants. Or use 4 to 5 pounds per 100 square feet.

Azaleas and camellias must be kept cool and moist in the hot months ahead with a mulch of compost or peat moss. Both of these plants must be kept moist at all times.

Begonia, Fern, and Fuchsia
Keep up the every-other-week feeding with organic fish fertilizer. (See **The Art of Fertilizing,** *March.*) Increase watering now. Mulch the beds as temperatures soar. (See **The Art of Mulching,** *February.*)

Feed tuberous begonias once a week until August.

Chrysanthemum
Keep pinched back, by the removal of terminal leaf buds, until August. (See *May,* "Do It Now.") Keep them anywhere between 6 and 12 inches high now.

Dahlia
Disbud dahlias if you are interested primarily in large blooms. Otherwise, settle for quantity rather than size. To disbud, nip off side buds in favor of one top bud.

Iris, Bearded
Divide them this month or next, as a general rule. (However, in the hot interior valleys division can be delayed until October.) If you have a substantial group of irises to divide, it's easier to do part of the job this month and part in July.

Dig the entire clump with a spading fork. Shake off the soil, or wash it off, and gently pull the rhizomes apart. (*Rhizomes* are conversational Gardenese for the thick underground stems or rootstocks.) Or several of the outer rhizomes can be left joined, and planted as a group. The old rhizomes in the center, which have no foliage, should be discarded. Cut the foliage back, straight across, leaving a stand of about 3 inches. While you are replanting, it's a good idea to do a temporary labeling job by scratching the name or color on the foliage, with a nail.

Iris is a one-way grower, so the growing end must be headed in the direction you want it to spread. Several rhizomes planted individually, but heading toward one another, would be on a collision course. Replant them as quickly as possible so that the new roots will have good moist earth to find their way in. Work the soil thoroughly beforehand, adding compost and bone meal to a depth of a foot, but barely cover the rhizomes so that they are just below the surface.

Primrose

Divide primroses now, where they have become crowded. (See *January*, "Primrose.")

Roses

These need their monthly meal of rose food. Be sure to water the granules in thoroughly. Deep-watering is of increasing

---

THE ART OF CUTTING ROSES FOR BOUQUETS

Here are a few tips from the experts. Cut them late in the afternoon or early in the evening. NEVER cut them in the heat of the day. If you can't do it late in the day, then early in the morning will do. Always cut the stem on the slant, preferably just above a five-part leaf. The bud located at the axil (conversational Gardenese for the point where the branch diverges from the stem) will send out new shoots and ultimately produce additional blooms.

Split the bottom of the stem about half an inch. This enables it to take up moisture quickly.

To extend their indoor life, immerse roses in cold water up to the flower heads for several hours (all night, when they are cut in the late afternoon or evening).

Cut floribundas when one or two in the cluster are partially open.

When cutting blooms from climbers, wait until two or three petals are just opening from the bud.

importance now for roses. The soil should be moist to a depth of from 4 to 6 inches when you finish your deep-watering stint. Let the hose (preferably with one of the water-breaker types of nozzles such as the rose bubbler or water wand) lie in the basin of soil around the plant, with the water running slowly so that there is no runoff.

LET'S GET GROWING

Agapanthus (Lily-of-the-Nile)

This plant can give your garden a touch of classic beauty, blooming from June through August. The dark green, straplike foliage does not die back but is attractive all through the year. The plants are available

EASIER WAYS TO WATER

Watering tools are just as important as watering techniques. The following are moderately priced and available at most garden centers and some hardware stores:

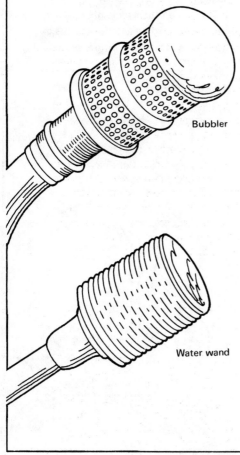

Bubbler

Water wand

Bubbler or Rose-Soaker. Allows a large volume of water to flow with a minimum of washing. It differs from the water wand in that it permits a heavier flow. One type has a valve to control volume—low, medium, or high. This is designed primarily for roses or any other plant that needs deep watering. It's excellent too for flushing out alkaline salts that build up in the soil.

Fogger. This one gives moisture in a super-fine spray. Seedlings benefit especially, since it waters without pressure on delicate stems and foliage. There is one called a seedling nozzle, also, but the fogger accomplishes the same thing. It's ideal for the humidity-loving plants, for overhead watering on hot days.

Water Wand. This long (4 feet plus) slender tube is well named, because it's magic when it comes to making problems disappear. Attaches like any other nozzle. Use it for those hard-to-reach spots. Or lay it on the ground and let it water gently at the base of a plant. It gives a soft flow, does not wash away mulch or precious top soil, and saves you a lot of bending down since it has a long reach.

Extension Rod. This is the perfect tool for watering hanging baskets. Similar in design to the water wand, it is curved at the end—no more

now at the nurseries, in gallon cans. The two names are used interchangeably.

Splendid as a background plant, equally stunning in containers on the patio, or marching beside a path, it bears clusters of trumpet-shaped flowers of varying tones of blue, and also white. Agapanthus orientalis is the tall one, the stems rising to 4 feet or more, with clusters of from 40 to 100 flowers. A. Africanus is smaller, no higher than 2 feet, with correspondingly smaller flower clusters.

Tips to Make You Tops with Agapanthus
1. This plant wants a loamy, well-drained soil. Dig the hole deeper and wider than

splashdown! Combined with the sweeper nozzle, it can double as a sweeper for patios and driveways.

Water Rod or Root Feeder. This combines watering and feeding, if desired. Between 3 and 4 feet long, it gets at the root of things. Push it down into the ground near the plants requiring deep watering. A jar attaches so that plant food may be added.

Extension rod
with fogger nozzle

Soaker-Sprinkler. One of those basic pieces you can't do without, once you've used it on narrow strips of ground not served by underground sprinklers, or on curving beds and borders. It is a perforated hose, either plastic or canvas, with tiny holes that deliver the water in gentle driblets at low pressure, or in soft spray at high pressure. Lay it along a hedge and leave it there during the summer months and into fall. All you have to do is to attach it to the hose when watering is needed. I use several in that way along borders and under shrubs. They come in 25- and 50-foot lengths.

Lawn Sprinklers. There are many choices, designed to cover almost any size or shape. Some have dials, for long, narrow, square, or round areas. They have a choice of distances, too—20, 30, or 40 feet.

Soaker-sprinkler

the size of the plant as it comes from the gallon can. Work in compost or peat moss and a handful of bone meal. Water well and let it settle overnight.

2. The location should be a sunny one, for maximum bloom, in the coastal and inner coastal areas; but it will need partial shade, especially in the afternoon, in the hot inland sections.

3. The tuberous roots can absorb large quantities of water, so water it regularly. Deep-water at least once a week in the months when it is in bloom and in bud, from spring through most of the summer.

4. Feed once a month with a 10-10-10 fertilizer until buds begin to set, then change to a low-nitrogen fertilizer.

5. Agapanthus will do well in the same place for as long as six years. It even seems to bloom more freely when it's crowded. However, when you want to move it, November and December are the best months. (See *December* for instructions, under "Do It Now.")

6. Plant it any time of the year from the gallon cans. Root divisions however, must be set out in the cool months.

Begonia, Tuberous

This is the glamorous one—colorful, varied, and almost indescribably beautiful. It is a little tricky to grow, in the hot inland areas, but worth every ounce of care you give it.

There are no named varieties, because tuberous begonias hybridize so readily that it would be virtually impossible to keep up with all of the new developments. Colors include yellow, orange, salmon, rose, pink, red, and white. The flower forms are enchanting: Picotees have white petals tipped or edged with pink or rose; pendulous types have double ruffled blooms; some,

such as the double-camellia types, resemble camellias and roses; others look like large carnations. (No wonder it's nicknamed "mockingbird flower"!)

If you can grow fuchsias in your area, you will be able to grow tuberous begonias. They want cool nights and thrive in the "fog belt" of the coastal sections. Inland gardeners have to create and maintain a humid environment, which may involve lath houses and misting devices, where night temperatures go to 65 degrees and higher. In that situation, it's really simpler to settle for the Bertini hybrids. They are less spectacular, but very beautiful.

Tips to Make You Tops with Tuberous Begonias

1. Plant them where they are protected from wind. They need partial shade (the American Begonia Society recommends from 50 to 60 percent shade), but not complete shade, or the blooms will be sparse. Filtered sun is good, but remember—sun at noon will spell doom!

2. There are two planting methods:

□ Start the tubers in damp peat moss or leaf mold, covering the entire surface of the tuber with the planting medium, about 1 inch thick. Be sure the container, whatever the type, has adequate drainage, since the planting medium must be kept damp. When leaves appear, transfer the young plants to their permanent bed. Soil must be rich and crumbly, much like that of a fern bed. Enrich it with compost or leaf mold. The leaves must face forward, since that is the direction the blossoms will face— the same direction as the foliage.

□ Start the tubers where they are to grow, and when the leaves appear, if they are not facing forward, gently lift the young plant and turn it.

3. Feeding doesn't require any guesswork. Here is a plant that tells you when it's hungry. When the foliage is light green and crimping upwards as though asking for a handout, give it one; that's the signal for feeding. Fish fertilizer is excellent, or use a complete fertilizer such as 10-10-10 until the buds begin to form, then change to a low-nitrogen food. When the leaves are a dark green and crimp downward, don't feed. It's easy to remember how to feed a plant that communicates so plainly. Just remember the signals—light green and up: When do we eat? Dark green and down: Everything's fine!

4. Keep the soil moist, but don't water so heavily that it becomes saturated. Use a misting spray or fogger nozzle to generate humidity when the temperature is 90 degrees and over. (See **The Art of Watering,** *May.*) Aside from the overhead misting, watering should be done at ground level.

5. Never water this plant late in the day. Morning is best, leaving time for the foliage to dry off thoroughly before evening. The overhead spraying is the exception; once in the morning, once in the midafternoon, if possible.

6. Keep faded blossoms removed, to avoid mold. When picking or cutting the blossoms, leave the complete stem standing. This is a safeguard against stem mold; the stem will deteriorate before the mold (which starts as soon as the flower is picked) can reach the tuber.

Bells-of-Ireland

Ring in the summer with Bells-of-Ireland. Its all-green color, except for the tiny white flower deep within the "bells," contrasts coolly with the more colorful plants in the garden.

You can have a ball with the bells in flower arrangements, using them either fresh or dried.

To dry: Remove the leaves and hang the flowers by the stems in a dark, dry, airy place, until they are thoroughly dried out. Or stand them in a jar for the drying time.

Ground Rules. Average soil will suit these annuals, but they want full sun. They are slow to germinate, taking from three to four weeks. Sow seeds where they are to grow, since they don't transplant too successfully. Their long blooming period makes up for the slow start, and they are outstandingly durable as cut flowers.

Big Blue Lily Turf

This is one of those durable, set-it-and-forget-it perennials that can take care of a problem corner of the garden or fill out a section of the border. It manages to look good all year, since it is evergreen, with attractive, dark green, narrow foliage of fountain-like growth, 18 inches long. Flowers are a violet blue, in clusters of spires at the center of the graceful foliage. Beautiful! Why don't we see more of it?

Ground Rules. Get it now, in 5-gallon cans (it's a big one!) at the nursery. Set it in well-worked and well-drained soil, in full sun or partial shade. (When you set out plants bought in cans or containers from the nursery, place them in the ground with the crown—the area between the root and stem—just as it is in the container, whether high or low.) Water thoroughly, once or twice a week. After the flowers fade, they will produce attractive, small black berries. Big blue lily turf is fast-growing, too, and wonderfully easy to divide. (See *October,* "Do It Now.")

Fern

A ferny thing happened on my way to the tool house one day. I discovered that some sword ferns had crept through the lattice fence from the main garden and established themselves in a narrow strip of ground considered too damp and shady for any practical purpose.

Here was ground that rarely saw the sun because of a hedge of eugenia grown to tree size. Dank and clayey, slippery with moss, it seemed pretty hopeless from a gardening standpoint. Yet, with the sword fern to encourage me, I began working an area about 8 feet long, in a crescent shape, adding compost—lots of it—bone meal, and a little sand.

A year later, the sword ferns make a miniature forest against the fence and maidenhair fern is set out in irregular patterns around the crescent, close to the path of stepping stones. Fuchsias, begonias, and coleuses are interspersed with low-growing wax begonias—and all through the art of changing the soil structure, the bed is now rich, loamy, and well drained.

Ferns are ideally suited to our coastal and inner coastal sections and play an increasingly important role in landscaping. Although, strictly speaking, they are not "flowers," it would be a disservice to the reader to omit them from a Southern California garden book.

Here's how to win fronds. Ferns have few problems and few pests. Their chief enemies are too much sun and inadequate moisture. They are modest in their demands. They need moist, humusy, well-drained soil, and shelter from winds—and will go placidly along, increasing in numbers and in some cases in size, year after year.

June is a good time of year to start a fern dell. Part of the joy of a garden is sharing it with friends and family, but even the most sociable of us can at times feel oppressed by too much togetherness. A small fern dell can be a green and peaceful retreat. Add a bench or a comfortable basket chair and it becomes a private sanctuary for resting, reading, thinking—and savoring that scarcest of commodities in today's world, just being alone.

The following ferns are easily maintained and demand little special consideration:

Asparagus Plumosus. Called Asparagus fern, although it's related to the lily family, this non-fern can be coaxed out of its rambling, untidy habits in the garden. " 'Capture' it in a standing cylinder of wire," advises William Eckert, fern expert extraordinary and a ranger with the Los Angeles Department of Recreation and Parks. He uses a lightweight wire, such as chicken wire, to form a cylinder 12-18

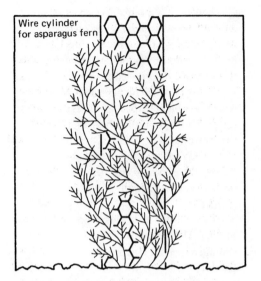

Wire cylinder for asparagus fern

inches in diameter. The fern winds its stems in and out, gradually spiraling upward until the wire is completely hidden by the delicate greenery.

Leather Fern. This fern gets its name from the glossy, leathery-textured fronds. It is ideal to use in combination with cut flowers, since it lasts up to six weeks in water.

Maidenhair. This is one of the most beautiful and easiest to grow of the ferns. The tiny, fan-shaped leaves and contrasting shiny, black stems are exquisite when mixed in with begonia semperflorens or at the base of fuchsias.

Mother Spleenwort. Called "mother" because it bears little bulbils, or pups, on the fronds, it is feathery and light green, with graceful arching fronds. The spleen-worts are particular about the crowns being set high.

Rabbit's Paw. This is a conversation piece because of its unique paw-like, furry "runners" or "feet," which are actually root-stocks growing along the surface of the soil. It is attractive in a fern bed but is more often used in hanging baskets.

Staghorn Fern. If you have a tree fern, you have the ideal place for a staghorn. This is an epiphyte—it subsists on air and water (which is living dangerously, in our polluted environment). In its native state it grows on the trunk of the tree fern. Start it on a batch of sphagnum moss bound with chicken wire. Attach the whole thing to the tree fern, and from then on all you have to do is water it once a day. Don't keep it soaked, or you will create a fungus condition that causes rot. The grayish green fronds resemble a stag's horn.

Sword Fern. This plant is so hardy and increases so rapidly, sending its runners in all directions, that it will take over unless controlled. It has a tendency to yellow if grown in dense shade. It will take full morning sun if it gets afternoon shade.

Tree Ferns, Australian and Tasmanian. Both will take sun for most of the day, as long as they are in a relatively sheltered location, in the coastal and inner coastal sections. Australian grows almost twice the height of the Tasmanian. The latter, which grows from 10 to 12 feet, is more suited to the average garden, but both are hardy and undemanding.

It's nice to have fronds in high places, too. Ferns are especially well adapted to hanging baskets. A combination of sphagnum moss, leaf mold and/or compost, sponge rock, and planter mix will give the best results. Line the container with the sphagnum moss, and let a couple of inches hang over until the planting medium is put in, then fold over the excess to prevent washing.

Tips to Make You Tops with Ferns
1. Give them a sheltered location with shade or filtered sun; loamy, well-drained soil.
2. Keep them moist but not soggy.
3. Feed twice a month with liquid fish fertilizer from May to November.
4. Sprinkle overhead when temperatures are over 90 degrees, early in the morning and in the late afternoon.

5. Plant close together to create the humid condition they need. They like to be surrounded by fronds.
6. Water ferns in hanging baskets oftener than those in beds. If the container is the open wire or redwood slat type, apply the water at the sides to give better penetration and distribution.

Gloriosa Daisy

This plant has come up in the world since the days it was called a plain old black-eyed Susan. In the glorification process of hybridizing, it has acquired colors of orange and mahogany brown. There's even one variety called Irish Eyes, with a yellow-green center, so, strictly speaking, it's not black-eyed Susan any more.

Ground Rules. Get the bedding plants now. Give them full sun and a well-drained average soil. You will be rewarded with an abundance of bloom all summer and well into the fall. You will also have a steady supply of cut flowers, from just two or three plants. Allow from 12 to 18 inches between each plant.

Zinnia

This hot-weather annual doesn't want to get growing until the ground has warmed up and night temperatures are staying above 50 degrees.

The zinnia is a long-lasting cut flower with an almost unrivalled color range. There's even a green one, appropriately named Envy. For garden color, stamina in the long hot days ahead, and a continuous supply of flowers for the house, this is the one! Plant half the packet of seeds the first week of June, the other half at the end of the month.

Zinnias are available now as bedding plants, but also easy and fun to grow from seeds (roughly a month and a half from sowing to picking).

Sow them outside where you want them to grow, if the night temperatures are staying above 50 degrees. However, they transplant well, so they may be sowed in flats.

The rather harsh colors and stiff forms of the old-fashioned zinnias have been modified and glamorized to the point where just about any height, color, and flower size can be grown.

Try California Giant and State Fair for the dahlia-flowered form. Zenith and Burpeeana have shaggy, quilled petals. Peter Pan and Cupid are low-growing, front-of-the-border types.

Tips to Make You Tops with Zinnias
1. Give them a sunny location, with average soil (but they will do even better with a soil that is well-worked, with manure added).
2. Space them to allow for good ventilation—at least 12 inches apart—since mildew is one of their few problems.
3. Irrigate, don't water overhead; damp foliage encourages mildew.
4. Keep them picked to encourage freer blooming.
5. Let the flowers open fully before cutting for bouquets; development stops quickly after they are cut.

FOUR BEAUTY SPOTS FOR JUNE PLANTING

Be your own landscape architect! Here are four suggested combinations of plants with similar sun, shade, soil, and moisture needs. These small adventures in the use of color and form are designed to beautify problem areas or to brighten up dull sections of the garden. Start with these, then try working out some of your own designs.

NAME	HEIGHT (INCHES) & SUGGESTED COLORS	SUN/SHADE	SOIL
Seeds:			
Dwarf Marigolds	12, yellow	Sun	Average
Painted Tongue	24-36, mixed (muted gold, red, bronze)	Sun	Fertile
Seeds:			
Bells-of-Ireland	24, green, touch of white	Sun	Average
Nasturtiums	8-12, mixed	Sun	Average
Bedding Plants:			
Along the walk, alternate clumps of:			
Campanula Porten-schlagiana	4-7, blue (evergreen foliage)	Sun, partial shade	Fertile, well drained
Coral Bells	12, coral (evergreen foliage)	Sun, partial shade	Fertile, well drained
Seeds: "Circle of Zinnias"			
Tall: California Giant	24-30, mixed	Sun	Average
Medium: Peter Pan	14, mixed	Sun	Average
Dwarf: Thumbelina	6-10, pink, salmon	Sun	Average
Dwarf Pompon	6-10, mixed	Sun	Average

Ensure adequate ventilation by spacing center zinnias roughly 12 inches apart; those in outside rows, 6 inches apart.

OTHER PLANTABLES FOR JUNE

Here are additional plants that may be started this month. The planting information will be found in the chapters indicated below by month. Unless otherwise stated, reference is to "Let's Get Growing" section.

SEEDS

Anchusa	*May "Beauty Spots"*	Marigold	*April, July; also March "Beauty Spots"*
Chrysanthemum	*March, May, June, July*		
Cockscomb	*July; also April "Beauty Spots"*	Mignonette	*January "Beauty Spots"*
		Nasturtium	*March*
Cosmos	*May "Beauty Spots"*	Pansy	*October*
Dahlia	*April, June, July, November*	Portulaca	*August*
Kochia	*July*	Sunflower	*April*
Larkspur	*May "Beauty Spots"*	Sweet Alyssum	*August, November*

BEDDING PLANTS

Ageratum	*April*	Gazania	*August*
Aster	*July*	Geranium	*April*
Baby's Breath	*July, also April "Beauty Spots"*	Gloriosa Daisy	*June*
		Marguerite	*March; also July "Beauty Spots"*
Campanula	*July, August; also March "Beauty Spots"*		
		Marigold	*April, July; also March "Beauty Spots"*
Carnation	*January*		
Chrysanthemum	*March, May, June, July*	Petunia	*March; also April "Beauty Spots"*
Coleus	*March, October*		
Coral Bells	*July, September; also June "Beauty Spots"*	Portulaca	*August*
		Salvia	*May "Beauty Spots"*
Cosmos	*May "Beauty Spots"*	Sweet Alyssum	*August, November*
Dianthus	*May "Beauty Spots"*	Verbena	*January; also March "Beauty Spots"*
Gaillardia	*January; also July "Beauty Spots"*		

BULBS

Dahlia	*April*	Gladiola	*February, May*

July

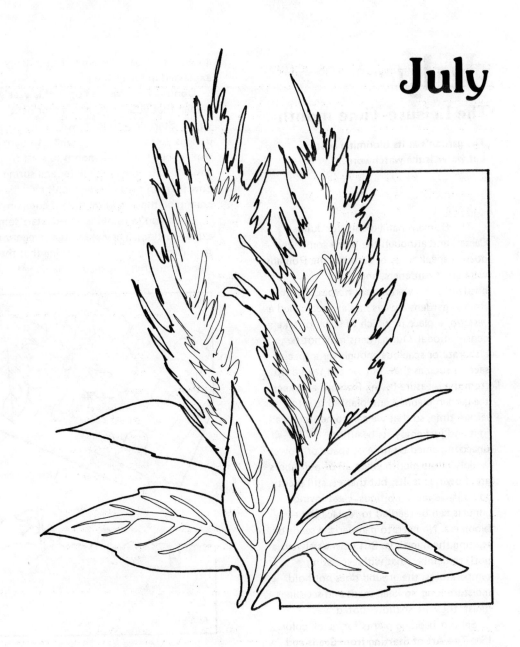

Plant of the Month: Feather Cockscomb. This glowing annual has dash and durability; the colors are brilliant gold, crimson, or pink. Long-lasting and heat resistant, the feathery, plumelike blooms are expressive of the plant's romantic nickname, "Plumed Knight."

July

The Leisure-Time month

**The garden's at its blooming best,
but water is the watchword.**

The Romans named July for Julius
Caesar, and although the name somehow
doesn't speak to us of gardens, the Romans
were great gardeners, and their
horticulturists were minor heroes. Formal
Roman gardens always had an area called a
gestatio, a place in which to stroll or take a
constitutional. Our gardens may not be
elaborate or spacious enough for a special
section such as that, but we can take a tip
from the pleasure-loving Romans and keep
the garden planned and planted to allow for
leisure time, so that we can sometimes walk
in it and just enjoy its beauties
unaccompanied by hose or spade or trowel.

July is the month when all of our labors
are showing results, but there is still plenty
to do if we feel ambitious. Heat-loving
annuals can be readied to replace the early
bloomers. No need to pamper the seeds by
starting them in flats. But (there's always a
but!) remember that with escalating
temperatures, the ground does not hold
moisture long, so keep seeds and seedlings
moist; they are shallow-rooted.

Set out bedding plants for quick color.
(See **The Art of Starting from Seeds and
Bedding Plants,** *January.*) Plant them late in
the afternoon, if possible. Although the
instinctive thing is to get at planting chores
early in the day, don't trust your instinct.
By setting out nursery-started plants late in
the day you are giving them a period of
adjustment, overnight. Otherwise, when the
sun gets to them they will wilt, and then the
growth is set back because of the energy
expended in readjusting.

Don't get so wrapped up in this year's
garden that you forget to plan for next
year's. Start now to jot down the colors and
designs you want to work with. It's hard to
realize, but this is the month to start sowing
annuals to bloom next winter and spring.
Sow them in flats, so you won't be
cramming them in with present company.

While you're thinking ahead, start some
azalea cuttings. They are in the category of
semihardwood cuttings, meaning that the
wood is not fully ripened or hardened.

Candytuft, Perennial

This perennial, often called *Iberis
sempervirens,* can be propagated now by
stem cuttings. (See **The Art of Propagation
from Softwood Cuttings,** *March.*) It can be
coaxed into a second round of bloom if it is
sheared back almost to the ground after
flowering.

THE ART OF SEMI-HARDWOOD CUTTINGS

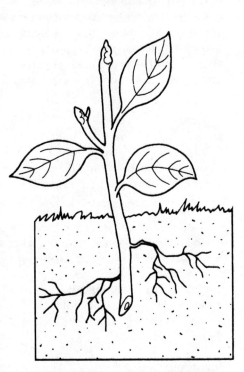

Six inches is a good overall length. Make a clean, slanting cut, one-quarter of an inch below a leaf or a pair of leaves, at the bottom end of the cutting, and one-quarter of an inch above a leaf or leaves at the top. Or use the tip of the branch as the top end.

Make a hole approximately 4 inches wide, 6 inches deep, and fill it with a mixture of half sand and half peat moss. The planting bed should be where the cuttings will not be overshadowed by other plants, or competing with them for moisture or soil nutrients.

Remove the leaves from the lower half of each cutting. Set the cuttings 2 or 3 inches deep. Avoid the all-too-common practice of making a preformed hole, since this can leave an air pocket at the bottom if the cutting doesn't go all the way down, and air space will encourage rot and fungus diseases.

Set the cuttings in place, and then water enough to settle the planting mixture around the cutting. Keep them moist, and transplant when they are well rooted (which means when you notice signs of growth, such as new leaf buds). Don't hesitate to take a cutting out of the ground to see how rooting is progressing.

Pot-in-Pot

You may want to use the pot-in-pot method rather than planting directly into the ground. Set a small (4-inch) pot with the drainage hole corked, into a larger (7- or 8-inch) pot. Fill the space between the pots with the above planting mixture and fill the small pot with water. (The small pot must be clay so that the water will seep through.) Insert the cuttings in the planting mixture, fairly close to the inner pot—and wait for them to root for you! The watering is automatically taken care of by the slow seepage of moisture through the sides of the small pot.

To check the progress of the cuttings, gently twist the inner pot and remove it; then reinsert gently.

Give the cuttings a soft, overhead sprinkling on hot days.

Perennials should be started now, to bloom next spring and summer. The important thing with both perennials and winter-blooming annuals is to get them established before the rainy season, and before night temperatures drop below 50 degrees.

Pinching Back

Chrysanthemum

This will begin setting buds next month, so July is the last month for pinching back. (See *May,* "Do It Now.") How high or low to keep the plant at this point is a flexible matter; anywhere from 4 to 12 inches is acceptable.

Dahlia

Dahlias should have a top dressing about this time. (See **The Art of Fertilizing,** *March.*) First fertilize with a mixture of one part steer manure, one part bone meal, one part bloom fertilizer (a complete fertilizer with a low nitrogen content such as 2-10-6). Apply the mixture well away from the base of the plant, at least 6 inches. About 10

pounds per 100 square feet is a good ratio. Water it in well. Next, apply a 2-inch mulch of compost, peat moss, or leaf mold. The mulch must be kept moist, especially if you are using peat moss, which tends to crust over in very hot weather if allowed to dry out. Give dahlias an overhead sprinkling occasionally to keep the leaves free of dust.

Delphinium

Keep the faded blooms of delphinium picked off. Feed now with liquid fish fertilizer, about a cup to a plant, pouring it around the base, never onto the crown. Water before and after fertilizing.

Fuchsia

Remove seedpods as soon as they appear. Fuchsias benefit from overhead sprinkling in hot weather, morning and afternoon.

Gerbera (Transvaal Daisy)

It should have a feeding of liquid fish fertilizer this month. Check the underside of the leaves for snails.

Impatiens

Impatiens *(Patient Lucy)* stores moisture in its stems, but it must have it in order to store it. Water it often—every other day or so—in the hot weather. (See **The Art of Watering,** *May.*)

Iris

Finish dividing bearded iris the first part of this month. (See *June,* "Do It Now" for method of dividing and replanting.) Inland gardeners can wait until September. Those that are not being divided (generally speaking, bearded iris can remain "as is" for two or three years) should be deep-watered every other week to encourage a second round of bloom in the fall.

Nasturtium

This should be kept picked, unless you are trying to accumulate the seed pods for

THE ART OF CARING FOR SPRINKLERS AND NOZZLES

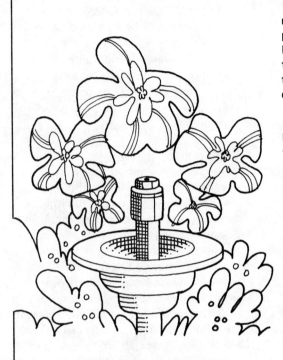

Off with their heads!—underground sprinkler heads, that is, if they are not performing properly. They may need cleaning. (It's easy, don't panic!) Some of the older types are not removable, but all that's necessary with the modern ones is to unscrew the center piece with the pliers, clean out the little holes, and replace. Clear away the grass, weeds, and any debris so that there is a 6-inch space around each head.

Some garden centers have little plastic discs that can be set over the heads to keep the surrounding area free of weeds or grass. If the sprinkler heads are too low, there are "risers" or extenders to raise them.

Keeping the heads in good condition and the surrounding area clear will give better water distribution and prevent the waste of water that just puddles in the immediate area if it's impeded.

Check the pulsating and twirling sprinkler nozzles that attach to your hose, also, to be sure they are operating properly. Little filters are available at most garden supply or hardware stores, to be inserted at the neck of the nozzles to keep out bits of gravel and other materials that can clog the mechanism. Most of the newer watering attachments come equipped with the filters.

pickling (see **Pickled Nasturtium Seeds,** *March*), in which case keep a small section separate to produce the pods and let the rest of the bed get glowing with color that lasts for months. Plant nasturtium seeds in the spaces between the newly divided and replanted iris to erase that rather bare look.

Pansy

Mulch pansies now with compost or peat moss, and keep them well watered. It's important to pick off the faded blooms. It's amazing how productive these small plants are, so don't let them go to seed. Feed pansies once a month with a low-nitrogen organic fish fertilizer.

Stock

Stocks going down? They are pushovers when it comes to wind or hard watering. Keep them staked with the slim, green bamboo stakes, fastening them loosely with raffia or twist-'ems. These garden "cosmetics" can make a lot of difference in the face your garden presents to the world, but they should be as unobtrusive as cleverly applied makeup. The slim, green stakes will blend in with the stems and foliage if they are set properly so that they don't tower over the plants.

LET'S GET GROWING

Baby's Breath, Annual

It may not look like much, by itself, but what a mixer! It's a diaphanous plant, bushy in a delicate way, with quantities of dainty white, pink, or rose flowers. It's effective as a "filler" in the beds and borders to soften the more substantial plants and sharper colors. It grows to 24 inches. A dwarf type grows to 12 inches. Seeds planted now will blossom in September.

Ground Rules. Prefers ordinary soil; a rich, fertile soil spurs it to rangy growth. It wants sun.

It is lovely in flower arrangements, either fresh or dried. To dry, hang it in an airy, and dark or shady place.

China Aster

Growing asters is no bed of roses. First, the bad news: They are subject to fungus diseases, root aphis, and a virus called "yellows." They are short-blooming (four weeks) and must not be planted in the same place two years in succession because of their susceptibility to fungus diseases that build up in the soil.

And now the good news: They are worth the trouble you have to take to avoid dis-asters. The color range is glorious: white, pink, red, purple, cloudy yellow. Heights range from 8 inches to 3 feet. The flowers have a diversity of forms: singles, doubles, pompon, quilled, and frilled.

Ground Rules. Bedding plants are available now. Set them 12 inches apart in fertile, well-drained soil. They need full sun,

except in the hotter inland sections, where they should have partial shade. Mulch with compost (not with peat moss—asters don't like the acidifying action).

Aster roots are shallow, so the taller plants must be staked. Be careful not to overwater. How much is enough is, of course, the perennial—and annual—problem. The simplest way to determine whether or not moisture is needed is to scratch down an inch or so into the soil. (See **The Art of Watering**, *May.*)

Coral Bells

Ring some changes on coral bells by alternating the coral-colored with white. This dainty evergreen perennial is lovely as an edging or as a ground cover under trees. Be careful how you use it with other plants, because its delicate bell-shaped flowers, rising on spires from tufts of foliage, can be somewhat overpowered by plants with larger, sturdier blooms.

Ground Rules. Set out the bedding plants this month, in loamy, well-drained soil, in sun or partial shade, about 8 inches apart. Water regularly; in the hot interiors, mulch with compost. (See **The Art of Mulching**, *February.*)

Dalmatian Bellflower (Campanula portenschlagiana)

One of the most versatile perennials around, it will grow in full sun, partial shade, and almost complete shade, yet produce clouds of violet-blue flowers in May and June, with a sprinkling of bloom right on through to early fall.

Ground Rules. Ample moisture is the key to success with this one. It will do well in rather indifferent soil as long as it is well drained. Height is from 8 to 15 inches, roughly.

It is the perfect edging plant and is equally effective as a ground cover. Increase it by division, any time before or after the height of the bloom period. It's a charmer in the patio, too, and in hanging baskets. As an edging plant, it should be spaced 8 inches apart.

Feather Cockscomb

This plant is long lasting, heat resistant, and doesn't care what kind of soil you plant it in as long as it gets plenty of sun. What more can you ask? But there *is* more: This durable annual (the flower lasts for almost two months) can be dried and used spectacularly in winter floral arrangements. To dry, hang it in an airy and dark or shady place. Incidentally, all flowers to be dried should be cut when they are looking their best.

Ground Rules. Although it will do well in practically any soil, feather cockscomb will be more productive in a fairly rich, well-drained soil that holds the moisture it loves. In a poor soil, mix in compost; in the inland areas, also mulch to hold moisture.

The more sun it gets, the happier it will be. Golden Fleece is the most adaptable color for combining with other plants, although, if you want to try the really gaudy shades, it's also available in deep crimson and pink. Space the plants about a foot apart. Sow the seeds now, and you will have long-lasting color in the garden, plus a stunning cut flower for indoors.

Geum

This evergreen perennial glows like a rose (which it resembles). Colors are red, yellow, and orange. Beautiful geums, how rarely we see 'em—and it's hard to understand why. They are good mixers; try them with blue lobelia or blue Japanese iris, or with pincushion flower. Bedding plants are available now. For variety, try these: Princess Juliana, semidouble, orange-bronze; Lady Stratheden, semidouble, golden yellow; Fire Opal, semidouble, scarlet; Mrs. Bradshaw, double, scarlet.

Tips to Make You Tops with Geums

1. Set them out in good, moist, well-drained soil, thoroughly augmented with compost or peat moss. They like full sun in the coastal and inner coastal regions, but need partial shade further inland. Space them a foot apart, and water them regularly and thoroughly.
2. Feed them in the spring with a balanced fertilizer such as 5-10-5. This should be followed by a once-a-month feeding with a bloom fertilizer throughout the summer.
3. Remove the faded flowers before they can produce seed. This is done, of course, to prolong the blooming period; however, seedpods of the geum are almost as attractive as the flower, so you might want to let some of them reach that stage.
4. Divide the clumps in the spring, every two or three years.

Kochia or Mexican Fire Bush

This is a fun plant, an annual that thrives in heat and has a dual personality: its compact but feathery foliage is green in summer and turns fiery red in the fall. Effective and distinctive as a divider or screen, it can be used as a temporary hedge and can be sheared back to the desired height. Its normal height is 2 to 3 feet.

It also makes an attractive accent plant, with its compact, globe-shaped form, by steps or paths, or in contrast with more conventional plants. This is primarily a foliage plant; the flowers are few and inconspicuous. Use Kochia as a container plant also, especially for balcony plantings, since it stands up well in windy locations.

Ground Rules. Plant the seeds now (they can be sown as early as March or April, outdoors), in average soil, in full sun. In two to three weeks when seedlings are 3 inches high, they can be thinned to 12 inches apart, to use as a hedge or divider, or 18 inches apart for use in beds and borders.

Marigold

It's not too late to plant marigolds; they'll be around until the first frost. (See Marigold, "Let's Get Growing," *April.*) You can plant from seeds—they're fast growers—but for something a little special, get bedding plants of the small "Nuggets" for front-row color, and "First Lady" for larger blooms and intermediate height (in between the African and the French). These two varieties produce no seed, and thus all their energy is channeled into bloom production. They cost a bit more, but it's fun to hoe a new row now and then, so experiment with different varieties, even if you try only a half dozen or so of each.

Moonflower

This perennial treated as an annual is a "scent-sible" one, a night-bloomer. Its botanical name, *Calonyction,* means "beautiful night." Strictly speaking it is a vine, but it is included here because of the exquisite white blossoms, which are approximately 6 inches in diameter, very fragrant, and especially glamorous when used in evening floral arrangements.

Ground Rules. While it's a fast grower, it's slow to germinate, so give it a little help by soaking the seeds until they have doubled or tripled in size. Plant them where they are to grow, as they don't transplant well. Space them a foot apart, and give them a trellis or just a string or wire to climb on. The flowers open after the sun goes down, the white remaining open until noon the next day; a lavender variety stays open only in the nighttime. All these flowers are heat lovers, so give them full sun in average soil. Water regularly, but don't keep them moist.

For use indoors, cut the just-unfurling buds. They will remain open until morning.

Combine with alternate plantings of morning glory; this gives you blossoms day and night.

FOUR BEAUTY SPOTS FOR JULY PLANTING

You can be your own landscape architect! Here are four suggested combinations of plants with similar sun, shade, soil, and moisture needs. These small adventures in color and style are designed to beautify problem areas or to brighten dull sections of the garden. Start with these, then try working out your own designs.

NAME	HEIGHT (INCHES) & SUGGESTED COLORS	SUN/SHADE	SOIL
Bedding Plants:			
Felicia	18, blue	Sun	Average
Marguerite	24-36, white, yellow	Sun	Average
Seeds:			
Feather Cockscomb	12-36, gold	Sun	Any
Zinnia	12-36, mixed	Sun	Average
Bedding Plants:			
Dusty Miller (Centaurea Cineraria)	10-12, grayish-white foliage, yellow flowers	Sun	Average
Gaillardia	18, orange, red, white, yellow	Sun	Any
Bedding Plants:			
Geum	18-24, scarlet	Sun, partial shade	Well drained
Candytuft, Perennial	8-10, white	Sun, partial shade	Well drained

OTHER PLANTABLES FOR JULY

Here are additional plants that may be started this month. The planting information will be found in the chapters indicated below by month. Unless otherwise stated, reference is to "Let's Get Growing" section.

SEEDS

Bells-of-Ireland	*June*		Painted Tongue	*June* "Beauty Spots"
Coleus	*March*		Portulaca	*August*
Cosmos	*May* "Beauty Spots"		Shasta Daisy	*May*
Gaillardia	*January;* also *July* "Beauty Spots"		Sunflower	*April*
			Sweet Alyssum	*August, November*
Marigold	*April;* also *March* "Beauty Spots"		Verbena	*January;* also *March* "Beauty Spots"
Nasturtium	*March*		Vinca Rosea	*May* "White Garden"
Nicotiana	*May* "Beauty Spots"		Zinnia	*June*

BEDDING PLANTS

Ageratum	*April*		Impatiens	*April* "Beauty Spots"
Balsam	*April* "Beauty Spots"		Marguerite	*March*
Begonia	*May*		Marigold	*April;* also *March* "Beauty Spots"
Candytuft, perennial	*April*		Nierembergia (Blue Cup Flower)	*April* "Beauty Spots"
Carnation	*January*		Petunia	*March;* also *April* "Beauty Spots"
Chrysanthemum	*March* "Do It Now"			
Coleus	*March*		Phlox	*May*
Cosmos	*May* "Beauty Spots"		Portulaca	*August*
Dianthus	*May* "Beauty Spots"		Salvia	*May* "Beauty Spots"
Felicia	*March;* also *July* "Beauty Spots"		Sweet Alyssum	*August, November*
Gaillardia	*January;* also *July* "Beauty Spots"		Verbena	*January;* also *March* "Beauty Spots"
			Vinca Rosea	*May* "White Garden"
Gazania	*August*		Zinnia	*June*
Geranium	*April*			
Gloriosa Daisy	*June*			

August

Plant of the Month: Iceland Poppy. The only poppy that transplants successfully, it warms the heart of winter with such vibrant colors as orange, salmon, rose, pink, white, and yellow. It's a long-stemmed, long-lasting cut flower, too.

August

The Water-Everything Month

Time for annual sprees and perennial pleasures.

August has an imperial background. It was named for the Emperor Augustus who favored the month because it was for him a time of good fortune and many victories. Of course, good fortune in the garden is not a matter of luck, but of care, and its victories are won in battles with heat and drought this time of year. We give a large part of our August gardening time to watering and soil conservation; protecting the garden against erosion is the big think-ahead subject for this month.

Keep an eye out for signs of the buildup of salts in the soil. Browning of leaf edges on garden plants and white chalky deposits on the rims of containers mean that it's time to take corrective measures.

Leach out the alkaline deposits by thorough, gentle watering to wash them down below the root zones. (Leach: conversational Gardenese for washing away or flushing out deposits.) Let the water run until the soil is thoroughly soaked. Set container plants on grass or gravel so that the water will run off freely; fill the pot to the brim, let it seep on down and out; then repeat about four times. Because some soil nutrients will be lost in the process of flushing out salt deposits, always follow leaching with a feeding of organic fish fertilizer. (Use just half strength for the container plants.)

The use of a good mulch now will help to keep moisture from evaporating quickly from the soil at the base of the plants. Compost is the best mulch for the purpose, but not everybody has a compost heap. (See **The Art of Composting,** *September.*) Peat moss is all right, if you observe certain precautions. (See **The Art of Mulching,** *February.*)

How to tell whether or not the soil is wet enough is one of the most-asked questions. C. E. Maier of Whittier raises cacti and succulents as a hobby, and watering at the proper time is one of the secrets of success with these plants. He bought an electronic gauge but wasn't satisfied with the results, so he devised his own.

He buys a 36-inch-length of balsa wood—one-eighth inch thick for the potted plants, one-half inch thick for ground use. These are cut into pieces approximately 6 inches long, with the ends sharpened. (He uses a pencil sharpener for the small size.) He inserts the end into the soil, and it immediately absorbs moisture, darkening the wood to whatever depth it has been placed. If it comes out dry, he gets to work with the watering pot. "I haven't used my electronic water gauge since I started using balsa wood," says Mr. Maier. "The wood is cheap—ten to fifteen cents for a 36-inch piece—fast, and reliable." His 200 pots of cacti and succulents aren't complaining, either. Buy balsa wood at hobby shops. (It's used in making airplane models, among other things.)

August is a good time to go on an annual spree; get ready for the trooping of the colors of winter- and spring-blooming annuals.

It's a time for sowing perennial pleasures, too. Perennials are the foundation of the garden, lasting for years. There is a dollars-and-sense advantage to growing them from seed; flats of bedding plants will cost anywhere from $7 on up, whereas seeds cost just cents per packet. For some reason

annuals outrank perennials in popularity to
the point where many nurseries stock only
a few perennials. Keep asking for your
favorites, but meanwhile start with seeds.
(See **The Art of Starting from Seeds and
Bedding Plants,** *January.*)

DO IT NOW

Azaleas and Camellias

Azaleas and camellias should have their
final feeding of the year (March, May, and
August are the three months) about the
middle of the month. The commercial azalea
and camellia food is excellent. It comes in a
dry granule form, which is scattered on the
soil around the plant, a tablespoon for each
foot of height. Be sure to water it well; a
fertilizer is effective only in solution.

Camellias should be disbudded this
month to promote larger blossoms. Of
clusters of three or four buds, remove two,
preferably a large and a small one. If you
leave only the larger buds, they will all open
at approximately the same time. Removing a
mixture of small and large buds yields a
progression of bloom.

Daisy

Divide Shasta daisies when they finish
blooming (some will be blooming into
October). Prepare the soil just as for the
daylilies, this chapter. Incidentally, if you
have no compost, peat moss, or leaf mold to
add as organic matter to improve the soil
structure, use a good planting mix. (Planting
mix should not be confused with potting
mix, which is of a finer texture.)

Crown gall is one of the few problems
afflicting shastas. It shows up as an irregular,
rough-surfaced growth on the crown, and
once you find it, you might as well dig the
whole plant up and dispose of it (not on the
compost heap), since there is no remedy. Dig
out a section of the soil immediately
surrounding the plant, too. This is a

soil-carried disease which can infect the
plant only through a cut or wound, so be
careful when digging around the Shastas.

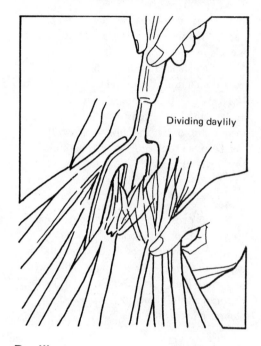

Dividing daylily

Daylily

Ordinarily this gorgeous, almost no-
problem plant can stay where it is for as
long as six years, but division is a good way
to increase your stock of favorites. Dig the
whole clump, including as much of the
roots as possible. Shake the loose soil off,
then wash the remainder off with the hose.
Gently pull the ramets apart. (*Ramets:*
Conversational Gardenese for sections.)
Some clumps will be tougher than others, so
use a knife and cut them apart if necessary.
Don't panic if you break off some pieces
with no roots; they can be rooted in sand,
using the same procedure you use for
cuttings. (See **The Art of Propagation from
Softwood Cuttings,** *March.*)

Replant right away, preparing the soil
thoroughly. Dig to a depth of a foot, and
work the soil until it is well broken up. Add
compost or peat moss if the drainage needs

improving; the soil may be too heavy or clayey, and one of the few demands daylilies make is for well-drained soil.

Add a balanced fertilizer, 5-10-5, and work it well into the soil (about 5 pounds to 100 square feet, or proportionately less for smaller areas). Divisions should be set into the ground so that the top, or crown (the area between root and stem), is an inch below the surface.

Roses

Give the roses some grooming now in preparation for fall blooms. Remove any crisscrossed branches or dead wood, and be regular in your deep watering. Fertilize with rose food. (See "Let's Get Growing: Roses," *February.*) And remember to keep dead blooms picked off.

LET'S GET GROWING

Calendula

This plant just about dares you to fail, it's such an easy grower. Keep the faded flowers picked off and you will have abundant cut flowers for the house and a sunshine look for any area in the garden that needs fast, long-lasting color.

In the cooler areas, sow the seeds directly where they are to grow; in the inland valleys, start them in flats.

Ground Rules. Calendulas are very undemanding as to soil and water, but want plenty of sun—six hours a day, preferably. Be sure to water your annuals thoroughly as you are setting out the seedlings or bedding plants to give them a good start. Calendulas are excellent container plants, too—one of their nicknames is "pot marigold." Colors most often seen are yellow and a bright orange gold, but they come also in apricot, cream, and lemon.

Foxglove

You can hardly find a more exuberant plant than this, growing to a height of 5 or 6 feet, with flower spikes as long as 2 feet, crowded with bell-like flowers in pink, purple, rose, white, and yellow.

Ground Rules. Give it moist, loamy soil in a predominantly shaded area, although it will grow in sun near the coast. Space the plants about 2 feet apart.

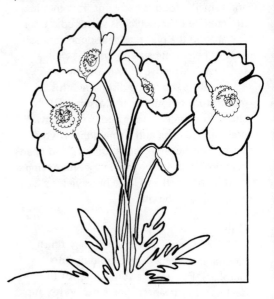

Iceland Poppy

If you had only one choice for a winter splash of color, this perennial treated as an annual would fill the bill. The colors are cream, orange, pink, rose, salmon, white, and yellow. The 3- to 4-inch blooms are borne on graceful 18-inch stems, and are ideal cut flowers. (Cut them in bud.) The stems should be seared to "seal" the ends, otherwise they emit a liquid that clogs the stem and prevents water intake. To sear: Apply a lighted match to the extreme end of the stem for perhaps two or three seconds, being careful to hold the stem at an angle so the heat of the flame won't damage the flower—or your fingers!

Ground Rules. Start the seeds in flats, in a good potting mixture, and sprinkle lightly with sand, to cover the seeds. Transplant to permanent beds when the seedlings are a sturdy 2 inches high. Don't kill them with kindness; like most poppies, these want a light, well-drained soil rather than a rich, loamy one.

Be sure they get plenty of water. They are thirsty ones; that's why a well-drained soil is important. Failure to keep them moist will result in blossom drop (conversational Gardenese for the condition that causes buds to fall to the ground without opening).

Stock

This flower gives you just about any color you want—a mix of yellow, white, pale pink, maroon, lavender, and purple—in singles and doubles, but predominantly doubles. (In Conversational Gardenese, singles denote flowers with a specific number of petals of a uniform size and shape. Doubles simply have more petals than the single form of the flower. Semidoubles are about midway between singles and doubles.)

Ground Rules. Sow the seeds late this month, in the coastal and inner coastal areas. Inland, wait until October. They transplant very successfully, so you might as well start them in flats unless you have plenty of planting space. Give them plenty of sun—about six hours a day, preferably—and average to fertile soil. They don't seem to care too much about the soil condition, but they insist on regular watering—every day in very hot weather—90 degrees and up.

Sweet Violet

This distinctive and poetic plant grows easily from seed, and once established it will reseed diligently. The seeds are borne in a capsule that, as it ripens, separates into three sections—narrow, curved, and boat-shaped. Drying creates almost a springlike reaction, catapulting the seeds away from the parent plant. Basically this is a woodland plant, so it thrives in shade, with filtered sun. It does well in the cool-summer regions, but the hot summers of the inland seem to promote excessive amounts of foliage, with few blossoms.

EAT YOUR PLANT AND HAVE IT TOO: VIOLET TEA

This is an epicure's delight, easy to make and rich in vitamin C. Back in Victorian days it was as common as crumpets, but today it's a rare treat.

Use the blossoms whole, the leaves shredded (or use just the leaves). Wash gently, then pour boiling water over them and let steep for 10 minutes. Try a proportion of two cups of water to each half cup of the leaves and flowers.

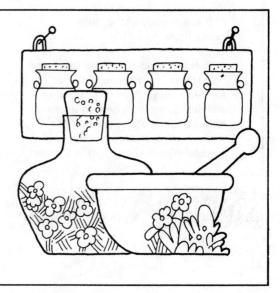

Ground Rules. Violets want a moist, loamy soil, even a little on the acid side. Dig some peat moss into the soil and keep the plants on the moist side—this seems to be the number one factor in producing abundant bloom. If you are planting from root divisions, set them with crowns (the area between the root and stem) close to the surface of the soil.

Once established, they will take care of

THE ART OF GROWING GROUND COVERS

August is a great time of year to start setting out ground covers. Not only are they attractive in their compact and often colorful growth, but they are labor savers (no mowing) and conserve soil and water.

In a day of shifting lifestyles, we like to think that land, at least, is a physically stable commodity that can't be lost. That's not quite the case, however.

While it's pretty unlikely that soil rustlers are going to sneak in under cover of night and make off with your front yard, soil can be lost through a number of natural processes, one of the commonest being that of erosion or runoff owing to heavy rains or hard watering.

With the rainy season still several months away, this gives us plenty of time to plan and plant ground covers. We are often rather unimaginative when it comes to selecting plants for this purpose, perhaps because we think of it as a remedy, rather than a horticultural happening. It can be both!

A few ground covers will take some foot traffic (conversational Gardenese for "you can walk on it"), but most will not. Some grow best on slopes or hillsides, while others (such as the heavy-headed, shallow-rooted succulents) will slide down in a heavy rain, taking the soil along with them. Some want shade, some want sun, or a combination of both.

Because many ground covers are easily increased by runners or root divisions, or both, you can cut the initial expense by starting small; thus a flat of gazanias will cover triple the original space within a year. Gazania and ajuga (carpet bugle) will start new plants from only a portion of a runner or a rooted piece, and never look back. That's part of the beauty of it— ground covers really cover ground!

Ground Covers for Problem Areas

Nature, in her lavish fashion, offers a ground cover for just about every situation, whether it is a sandy hillock at a beach home, a steep hill behind a canyon home, or just a problem area in the garden that isn't easily accessible for mowing.

Don't hesitate to use annuals as temporary ground covers while you are making up your mind about the right perennial. The bright colors of portulaca or the fragrant sweet alyssum can solve the problem of "in the meantime" plantings.

For a real adventure in color and contrast, and to learn some of the relative merits of various ground covers, try transforming a small area with combinations of compatible

their own reseeding, but if you have definite ideas about where you want them, save the little "boats" of seeds to plant in fall or spring. Sow them where you want them to grow by just working the soil and scattering the seed, covering with fine soil or potting mix, and firming them down.

Violets make excellent ground covers under trees and are also effective as edgings. Mine thrive near calla lilies and azaleas.

---

plants—for example, one of those narrow strips of lawn running down the center of a driveway or on either side. These are a nuisance to maintain as lawn, since they are hard to mow and usually too narrow to make sprinklers practical.

I had just such a problem area in the center of my driveway, from gate to garage. Rather than sticking to one type of plant, I have used a variety, in a series of 3-foot planting beds.

As a result, what was once a long, narrow, patchy-looking strip of grass is now a series of miniature beds, a long, eye-catching conversation piece.

First consideration was to find plants of the same height—no higher than 4 inches, to allow the car to pass over them without scraping the tops of the plants. Second was the matter of sun, shade, and moisture requirements of the various types of plants. Obviously, ajuga, which I wanted in the shady section and which is a shade and moisture lover, couldn't be planted next to sun-loving gazania, which is happy in a rather dry soil.

The final design has ajuga at the end, in the shade of the elm tree, herniaria next to it (the Greeks named it; they considered it a cure for hernia; its nickname, rupturewort, isn't much of an improvement either), and a double bedding (6 feet rather than 3)

of gazania, not the hybrids, but the low-growing gazania splendens. Adjoining the gazania is the one annual in the bunch, sweet alyssum (Royal Carpet and Carpet of Snow). This reseeds so effectively that it is as good as a perennial.

Be sure, in this type of level planting, that the heights are approximately the same. I made the mistake of planting portulaca in one of the beds, but found it too high to be practical for a center-of-the-driveway location; and, in addition, its sprawling habit takes away from the solid, carpet effect of the other ground covers used.

The following chart lists 15 ground covers for a variety of situations. All are plants that require little maintenance, and in some cases virtually none. Some are heat- and drought-tolerant.

Mother of Thyme is the most practical and undemanding of those listed here. It is the only one that will take foot traffic, and that should be limited. Use stepping-stones with a curb strip planting. It forms a solid, low-growing carpet, yielding a delightful aromatic fragrance when stepped on. It takes virtually no maintenance beyond an occasional watering, so thyme under your feet means time on your hands for other garden projects.

GROUND COVERS—LOW (OR NO) MAINTENANCE

NAME	CHARACTERISTICS	SUN/SHADE	FLOWER	USE
Ajuga	Dark green foliage, carpet effect.	Shade, or filtered sun	Blue	On slopes or level.
Baby's Tears	Minute, light green foliage. Holds moisture, can be used as "living mulch."	Shade	None	Slopes or level; living mulch for camellias
Candytuft, perennial Evergreen (Iberis Sempervirens)	Always attractive.	Sun	Snowy, long-blooming	Anywhere
Cinquefoil (Potentilla Cinerea)	Foliage resembles strawberry leaves; fast-growing, thrives in poor soil.	Sun or shade	Tiny; yellow	Slopes or level; under trees
Dalmatian Bellflower (Campanula Portenschlagiana)	Attractive heart-shaped foliage; evergreen, fast-growing.	Partial shade	Star-shaped; blue; blooms from May-July	Many uses; under trees, along walkways
Evergreen Candytuft (Iberis Sempervirens)	Low-growing, always attractive.	Sun	Snowy, long-blooming	Anywhere
Gazania (Gazania Splendens)	Durable, fast-spreading, heat- and drought-tolerant.	Sun	Daisy-like; orange, white, pink, red, yellow	Ideal for narrow strips, parkings (curb strips), driveways
Herniaria	Low, tight-growing carpet effect. Foliage turns red-bronze in winter.	Sun	Greenish; minute	Carpet bedding, parkings (curb strips), driveway edgings
Hottentot Fig	Fast-growing, heat-and-drought tolerant.	Full sun	Rose, yellow	Ideal for hillsides, sandy slopes, beach homes
Ivy Geranium	Fast-growing; ivy-shaped	Sun/shade	Double; pink,	Slopes or level
Japanese Spurge	Fast-growing, attractive foliage; evergreen; wants acid soil.	Shade	White; fragrant	Slopes, under trees, driveway strips
Mesembryanthemum	Heat- and drought-tolerant. Fast-growing; gray-green foliage.	Full sun	Small; lavender-rose; May-July	Blanket of color, in bloom.
Periwinkle (Vinca Minor)	Evergreen; thrives in poor soil.	Part shade	Small; blue	Slopes, under trees
Sea Pink	Grassy clumps.	Sun	Pink	Sandy slopes
Thyme, Mother of	Flat, close-growing, dark green aromatic foliage; very fragrant when stepped on.	Sun	Purple; June-Dec.	Dry, light soil; stands some traffic.
Trailing Lantana	Fast-growing, hardy.	Sun	Dense bloom; lavender-pink	Slopes, hillsides, walls

THREE BEAUTY SPOTS FOR AUGUST PLANTING

Be your own landscape artist! Here are three suggested combinations of plants with similar sun, shade, soil, and moisture needs. These small adventures in color and style are designed to beautify problem areas or to brighten dull sections of the garden. Start with these; then try working out your own designs.

For the first combination—coleus and baby's tears—buy the latter in a flat, and use a can or jar to cut it out in circular sections. When the coleus has been interplanted (conversational Gardenese for planting between), keep the baby's tears pulled away from the stems of the coleus. Baby's tears used in this way is a type of "pattern planting," and it is just as effective alone.

NAME	HEIGHT (INCHES) & SUGGESTED COLORS	SUN/SHADE	SOIL
Bedding Plants:			
Baby's Tears	2-3, tiny, light green foliage	Shade, filtered sun	Light, well drained
Coleus	6-24, multihued foliage	Shade, filtered sun	Light, well drained

Both of the above are used for their foliage. Flowers are inconspicuous. Use the baby's tears for this planting in circular sections, with the coleus interplanted. Circles of baby's tears should be about 3 inches in diameter. This charming ground cover spreads easily, so keep the little circular plantings groomed by pulling out the excess.

NAME	HEIGHT (INCHES) & SUGGESTED COLORS	SUN/SHADE	SOIL
Seeds (Miniature Bed):			
French Marigolds, Dwarf	6-8, brownish red, yellow	Sun	Average, well drained
Tom Thumb Zinnias	7-8, mixed (yellow, red, white, etc.)	Sun	Average, well drained

NAME	HEIGHT (INCHES) & SUGGESTED COLORS	SUN/SHADE	SOIL
Seeds:			
Nasturtiums, Dwarf	6-12, yellow, single	Sun	Average
Strawflower	24, mixed (pink, yellow, rose, purple, white, orange)	Sun	Average

Strawflower is excellent for dried bouquets. Cut just before fully opened (centers should be just starting to open). Hang upside down in a cool, dry place.

OTHER PLANTABLES FOR AUGUST

Here are additional plants that may be started this month. The planting information will be found in the chapters indicated below by month. Unless otherwise stated, reference is to "Let's Get Growing" section.

SEEDS

Baby's Breath	*July*	Gaillardia	*January;* also *July* "Beauty Spots"
Bells-of-Ireland	*June*		
Calendula	*November*	Larkspur	*May* "Beauty Spots"
Candytuft, Annual	*April*	Nicotiana	*May* "Beauty Spots"
Chrysanthemum	*March* "Softwood Cuttings"	Painted Tongue	*June* "Beauty Spots"
		Pansy	*October*
Coleus	*March*	Phlox	*May*
Coreopsis	*May* "Beauty Spots"	Viola	*September* "Beauty Spots"
Cosmos	*May* "Beauty Spots"	Zinnia	*June*
Dahlia	*April*		

BEDDING PLANTS

Begonia, Fibrous	*May*	Marigold	*April;* also *March* "Beauty Spots"
Coleus	*March*		
Gloriosa Daisy	*June*	Zinnia	*June*

September

Plant of the Month: Freesia. Here's a native South African that loves Southern California's climate so much it will come back year after year. Planted now, it will be blooming by February in a glory of color and fragrance that will last through March. Wonderful as a cut flower, too.

September

The Festive Month for Planting

Shorter days mean shifting sun and shade. Time for soil-searching.

September (meaning "seven," because it was the seventh month of the Roman year) was the festival month of Ceres, goddess of agriculture. Certainly it is a festive time for Southern California gardeners. Just looking at the list of seeds, bedding plants, and bulbs for this month gives you that "It's great to live in Southern California!" feeling.

There's a shade of difference in planting sun lovers beginning around the 23rd of the month. That's when the autumnal equinox occurs; for a 24-hour period, day and night are the same length. (*Equinox* means "equal night.") After that, consider it fall, officially. Shorter days are a little tricky for gardeners. Beds that were flooded with sun in the summer may have so much shade in fall and winter that sun-loving plants will refuse to grow. Watch planting areas from day to day now, and note the change in the amount of sun each receives. The best way is to jot it down in a garden notebook for future planting guidance.

Fall or not, we get some of our hottest weather this month. Keep up a watering schedule. (See **The Art of Watering**, *May;* **Easier Ways to Water**, *June.*)

Do a little soil-searching before you get at the fall planting in earnest. Take some thought for preparing the ground. Has the soil in your garden had any real renovating done in the past several seasons? If not, this is the time! If you have compost on hand, you are lucky, and so is your garden. (See box, **The Art of Composting**.) If you have

used it all up, use peat moss or leaf mold (although I don't like to think what the latter will cost; but at least the price may spur you on to starting a compost heap if you aren't already blessed with a sense of humus).

The equivalent of a fertilizer sack full of either of the two above amendments, plus 10 pounds of superphosphate or bone meal, will be the gift with a lift where your garden is concerned. This amount applies to an area of roughly 500 square feet.

Turn the soil over to just a spade's depth, and mix in all the materials; rake it smooth, water thoroughly, and then just let it settle for a couple of days. (It's a good idea to water the area you will be digging the day before to soften the soil and help it absorb the nutrients more readily.)

Take beds and borders a few feet at a time, and work in the amendments such as peat moss, leaf mold, or compost. You don't have to be broad of shoulder and strong of muscle with this little-by-little type of soil preparation. With a soft kneeling pad and a good trowel, you can work wonders!

DO IT NOW

Amaryllis

The bulbs should be divided before the leaves make their appearance. (Amaryllis blooms before foliage appears, sending up a tall, bare stalk, which accounts for its nickname of "naked lady.") Dig the bulbs carefully, shake off the soil, and replant at once. Contrary to most bulbs, this one should be planted so close to the surface that it shows a bit through the soil. The one thing it is fussy about is being moved at the wrong time, and will take as long as four years to get over the sulks, during which time it refuses to bloom. So move it now. On the plus side, it is the most durable of bulbs, and you just may have it for the rest of your life: the lifetime of this bulb is 40 to 75 years.

In placing it, keep in mind that the long, straplike leaves take up a lot of room, since they can sprawl as far as 3 feet. For this reason it is best to plant it where it can't interfere with, or overshadow, less obstreperous growers. It isn't particular about soil, likes sun (it's drought-resistant), and will take light shade. It does not have to be divided every year (nor lifted and stored). Leave it where it is until the bloom begins to look sparse, which means it's getting overcrowded.

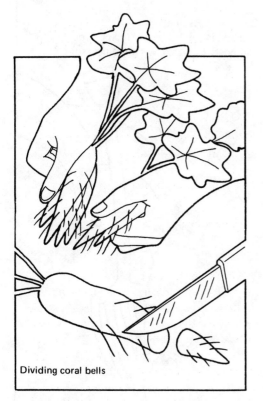

Dividing coral bells

Coral Bells

These should be divided now, if they have not been divided for the past three or four years. This friendly native thrives in all of the Western states, in shade or sun. (See "Coral Bells," *July.*)

Iris, Bearded

Inland gardeners should divide their bearded iris now. (See *June,* "Do It Now" section.)

Roses

Deep-water roses in this hottest of hot months, then fertilize, using either a commercial rose food or steer manure. A 2-inch top dressing of the latter works wonders. (See **The Art of Fertilizing,** *March.*)

LET'S GET GROWING

Butterfly Flower

Also known as poor man's orchid and schizanthus, this plant is one of the most colorful and distinctive of the cool weather annuals, and is a good one to include in your annual spree. Full flowering, with bright green, fernlike foliage, it has 1½- to 2-inch blossoms, usually bicolored, sometimes with just two different tones of one color.

Ground Rules. These are slow starters, so be patient—perhaps as long as a month. Start the seeds now, in flats, then plant a second and third batch at two-week intervals. They are noted for profusion of bloom but are not particularly long-blooming, and planting

THE ART OF COMPOSTING

Turning over a new leaf is not nearly as important for the garden as turning over old ones. Stop throwing away those leaves, lawn clippings, and kitchen scraps! Put them to work in the garden. If you have a sheltered, secluded spot where winds won't disturb the pile, and where there is partial shade so that the materials will not dry out easily, you have a place for a compost heap.

A simple one can be made of leaves piled up and watered and turned occasionally, but you'll get more substantial results if you add other ingredients.

There are several methods of composting, and each has its enthusiastic supporters. There are surface composters who build from the ground up; there are pit composters who start with a hole in the ground; there are composters who add chemicals to speed up the breaking-down process, and others who wouldn't think of it. Some confine the heap with boards, wire, or hollow brick; others just let it sprawl.

Compost "Recipe"

Here is a good basic "recipe" for compost: Leaves; lawn clippings; soil;

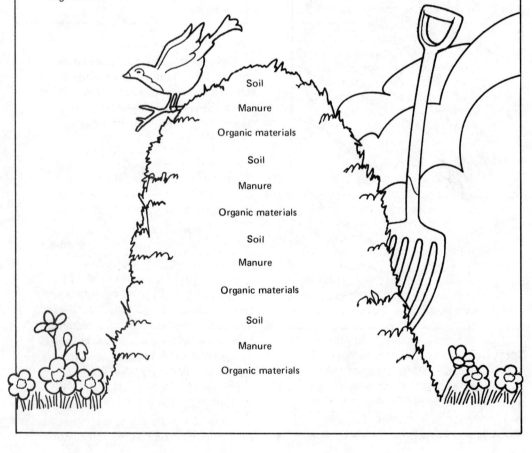

Soil

Manure

Organic materials

Soil

Manure

Organic materials

Soil

Manure

Organic materials

Soil

Manure

Organic materials

manure; kitchen scraps such as carrot tops, turnip and potato peelings, lettuce leaves, coffee grounds, various vegetable and fruit peelings, etc. The manure should constitute approximately a fourth of the materials. Add it to each layer.

Structuring is important—neatness counts! Make it in layers, alternating a 10- or 12-inch layer of organic materials such as the foregoing with 2-inch layers of plain garden soil. As you build it, the dimensions should be roughly 3 feet wide by 5 feet long.

Continue alternating the layers until the heap is at least 4 feet high. The pile must be a minimum of 4 feet in height, otherwise it won't generate enough heat to "cook" or break down the ingredients. However, 5 feet is about the maximum for convenience.

When it has reached the desired height, "cap" it by topping with 3 or 4 inches of soil. This is tantamount to shutting the oven door to keep the heat in.

Pile Should Be Turned

As the pile builds over the months, turn it now and then, perhaps once every six weeks. One way is to bring one end forward over the top, so that the contents are almost reversed. As the pile gets more substantial this is quite a job, so you may want to settle for aerating the pile: Poke the rake handle or any long stick into the pile here and there, or lift portions with a spading fork.

The whole point of turning or lifting the compost is to prevent it from building too much heat and losing nitrogen in the process.

It's vital to keep the pile moist. Dent the center slightly to let the water penetrate to the bottom. Moisture promotes the decomposition process, as do the microorganisms in the layers of soil.

There is no such thing as "instant compost," so don't expect to serve it to all those hungry mouths around the garden for at least six months. I give mine eight months, from September to May.

When it is ready—and you will know, because its ingredients will be so blended as to be indistinguishable—you will have a product so rich in humus that its value to your garden can hardly be overemphasized.

Humus: A Garden Treasure

Trying to describe *humus* is a waste of time. (Technically, it is partially or thoroughly decomposed animal or vegetable matter. All those microscopic organisms working away over the months have contributed nutrients practically impossible to acquire any other way.) Take a handful of that rich, black, crumbly, loamy-smelling substance and think of all the wonderful things it is going to do for your garden.

Work it into the soil; use it as a mulch; screen it for use as a potting mix. You will never want to be without it again.

One of the greatest things it will do for your garden is improve the soil structure. It breaks up or granulates heavy, compacted soil and at the same time it supplies nitrogen for the microorganisms that keep the soil "alive." Incidentally, a properly constructed compost never emits any odor.

them in a series will give a succession of bloom. When the seedlings are ready, transplant them to very humusy, moist soil, in semishade. When the transplanted seedlings have their second wind and are between 3 and 4 inches high, pinch back.

Don't underestimate the importance of pinching back; it can mean the difference, with many plants, between a one-stem plant with sparse bloom and a bushy, many-branched one with abundant bloom. (See **The Art of Pinching Back**, *April.*)

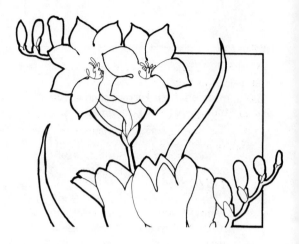

THE ART OF GROWING WILD FLOWERS

September is the time to start a wild flower garden. If you have thought of wild flowers primarily in terms of lupine and the California poppy (our State Flower), take a trip out to the Theodore Payne Foundation, 10459 Tuxford Street in Sun Valley, which is near Burbank (phone: 213-768-1802). You can see hundreds of varieties of native plants at this 22-acre garden site established to preserve and encourage the growing of California plants and wild flowers.

Seeds are available in quantities from 1 ounce to 1 pound.

Try the Rainbow Mixture to start with. It consists of 20 of the hardiest and showiest species, mixed to provide a succession of color and distinctive blooms from spring through late summer.

Ground Rules

For the annuals, dig the ground to about a spade's depth, and work the soil until it is pulverized; then rake the surface smooth.

Broadcast the seed (mixing it with sand will give it weight and also protect it from hungry birds), then water with a soft spray. After the seeds have sprouted, the rains will usually furnish all the moisture they need, but water them occasionally in the meantime if the season is unusually dry.

For the perennials, you have to work a little harder, since they don't reproduce as freely as the annuals. Start the seeds in flats, and follow the usual procedure of thinning and transplanting. (See **The Art of Starting from Seeds and Bedding Plants**, *January.*)

Freesia

Southern Californians are lucky to be able to grow this fragrant and colorful bulb outdoors. Once established, it will come up year after year, since it naturalizes (conversational Gardenese for adapting completely) here and asks for very little care.

Ground Rules. Plant freesias now and right on through to December, in light, well-drained soil where they will get plenty of sun. Plant with points UP. Set them 2 inches deep, 2 inches apart, and remember to water in these dry months of September and October. As a precaution against their taking a drubbing from heavy rains, plant a "cover" of alyssum or perennial candytuft. The shoots will pop up through that protective blanket and look even more sensational than they would alone. This bulb (actually a corm—an underground stem resembling a bulb, but lacking scales) doesn't need any precooling, and can stay where you plant it. Like most bulbs, it has a period of

The following is just a sampling of the multitudinous California wild flowers recommended by, and available at, the Payne Foundation.

VARIETY	HEIGHT (INCHES) AND COLORS	COMMENTS
Baby Blue Eyes	4-8, clear blue	Sun or shade, quick to flower
Blazing Star	24-36, deep yellow with ring of burnt orange	Sun or shade
Blue Lupine	12-24, deep blue	Likes a heavy soil, sun or shade
California Poppy	12-18, brilliant orange	Sun
Chinese Houses	12-18, white, lilac, rose	Prefers shade; flowers grow tier-on-tier, looking like little rows of houses
Clarkia	12-36, orchid pink	Full or partial shade
Gilia	18-36, bright blue	Excellent as cut flowers
Phacelia, large-flowered	24-36, lavender veined with violet	Sun; thrives in rather poor, dry soil

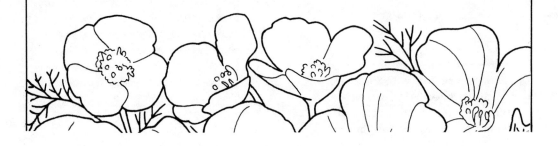

untidiness after blooming, but the ground cover more or less camouflages it. Let the foliage brown down before you cut it back.

The colors of freesias now include just about everything anyone could ask for: blue, orange, red, yellow, lavender, pink, white, and a few bicolors.

Snapdragon

Make it snappy with snapdragons; it's a race now between the first cold snap and the first bud. If the plants reach bud stage before cold weather (night temperatures below 50 degrees), they will bloom right on through the winter and into spring.

You have a choice of sizes—tall (3 feet plus), intermediate (to 18 inches), and dwarf (to 9 inches). And what colors! Rich, velvety crimson; deep red; rose; salmon; yellow; and white.

The Giant Ruffled, available in the intermediate size, is one of the wonders of horticulture. The size of the bloom is almost double that of the old-fashioned "giants." There is only one double snapdragon, the Supreme.

Tips to Make You Tops with Snapdragons
1. Beat the cold weather by setting out the bedding plants early this month, to promote midwinter-to-spring bloom.

(See **The Art of Starting from Seeds and Bedding Plants,** *January.*) Set them out late in the afternoon, in good, rich, composted soil, preferably where they will get full sun, although they will accept semishade. Space the tall from 18 inches to 2 feet apart; the intermediate and dwarf can be from 10 to 12 inches apart.
2. Water well when the plants are set out, but afterwards keep them on the dry side until strong growth begins.
3. Pinch back when they are adjusted to the shock of transplanting. (See **The Art of Pinching Back,** *April.*)
4. When the plants are about 10 inches high, feed with a bloom fertilizer (2-10-10) once a week. (See **The Art of Fertilizing,** *March.*)
5. When you have a color you would like to reproduce, snip off a cutting. It will root readily in sand or potting mix, and the color will come true.
6. You can give them a new lease on life if, toward the end of the blooming season, you shear the plants back to 6 or 8 inches. Feed with liquid fish immediately afterward. (The snapdragon is in the category of perennials grown as annuals.)
7. Rust is a snapdragon hazard, even though the plants you get at the nursery are usually from rust-resistant strains. (Check it out to be sure.) However, resistance to rust is no guarantee that the problem won't appear, since rust has a disconcerting habit of developing new strains. If rust shows up, pull up the plant and dispose of it at once (not on the compost heap). Here's how to recognize snapdragon rust: If you see chocolate brown powdery pustules (raised spots) on the leaf surface and yellowing of the upper surface, that's it.
8. Never water snapdragons overhead; it encourages dissemination of the rust spores.

FIVE BEAUTY SPOTS FOR SEPTEMBER PLANTING

You can be your own landscape designer! Here are five suggested combinations of plants with similar sun, shade, soil, and moisture needs. These small adventures in color and style are designed to beautify problem areas or to brighten dull sections of the garden. Start with these; then try working out your own designs.

NAME	HEIGHT (INCHES) & SUGGESTED COLORS	SUN/SHADE	SOIL
Seeds:			
Calendula	12-18, yellow, orange	Sun	Average
Fairy Star (Gilia)	6-8, red, yellow, white	Sun	Average
Viola	6-8, blue	Sun	Well drained
Bedding Plants:			
Butterfly Flower	18-24, pink, white, yellow, purple	Light shade	Moist, loamy
Fairy Primrose	8-12, pink, rose, lavender	Light shade	Moist, loamy
Bedding Plants:			
Snapdragon	36-48, pink, rose, crimson	Sun	Fertile, well drained
Stock (Giant Imperial)	24, white	Sun	Fertile, well drained
Seeds:			
Candytuft, Annual	8, pink, rose, lavender	Sun	Average
Sweet Alyssum (Carpet of Snow)	4, white	Sun	Average
Bedding Plants:			
Bergenia Crassifolia	12, lilac	Light shade	Loamy, moist
English Primrose	8-12, salmon, burnt orange, bronze	Light shade	Loamy, moist
Wax Begonia	6, white	Light shade	Loamy, moist

OTHER PLANTABLES FOR SEPTEMBER

Here are additional plants that may be started this month. The planting information will be found in the chapters indicated below by month. Unless otherwise noted, reference is to "Let's Get Growing" section.

SEEDS

African Daisy	*November*	Painted Tongue	*June* "Beauty Spots"
Baby's Breath	*July*	Pansy	*October*
Bells-of-Ireland	*June*	Petunia	*March*
Calendula	*August, November*	Phlox	*May*
Candytuft, Annual	*April;* also *September* "Beauty Spots"	Scabiosa (Pincushion Flower)	*July* "Beauty Spots"
Carnation	*January*	Shasta Daisy	*May*
Chrysanthemum	*March* "Softwood Cuttings"	Stock	*August*
Cineraria	*January*	Sweet Alyssum	*August, November*
Delphinium	*February*	Sweet Pea (bush)	*October*
Forget-me-not	*March* "Beauty Spots"	Sweet Pea (climbing)	*February*
Foxglove	*August*	Verbena	*January;* also *March* "Beauty Spots" and *September*
Godetia	*February* "Beauty Spots"		
Hollyhock	*February*		
Larkspur	*May* "Beauty Spots"	Viola	*October* "Beauty Spots"
Mignonette	*January* "Beauty Spots"	Virginia Stock	*November*
Nemophila	*October*		
Nicotiana	*May* "Beauty Spots"		

BEDDING PLANTS

African Daisy	*November*	Stock	*August*
Calendula	*August, November*	Sweet Alyssum	*August, November*
English Daisy	*February* "Beauty Spots"	Sweet Pea (bush)	*October*
Fairy Primrose	*January*	Viola	*September* and *October* "Beauty Spots"
Iceland Poppy	*August*		
Pansy	*October*		
Penstemon	*January;* also *April* "Beauty Spots"		

October

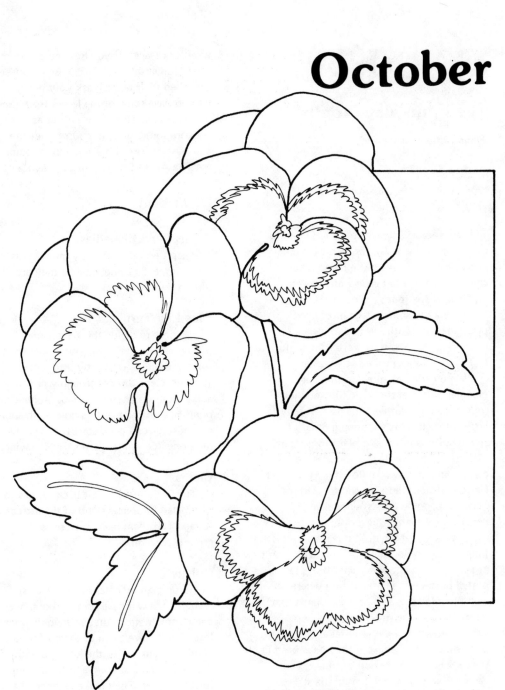

Plant of the Month: Pansy. The name is from the French word *pensée,* meaning "thought." So *think* of pansies—for bright blossoms looking like elfin faces; long periods of bloom; and many uses, including ground covers for bulbs, edging, bedding, and bouquets. Planted now, bedding plants will give abundant bloom by Thanksgiving.

October

The Four-Way Month

Plant (almost) anything!

In mythology, the entrance to Olympus, the home of the gods, was through a great gate of clouds at which the Seasons stood guard. Much of what we do this month partakes of the four seasons, and October is the gateway to some of the most exciting planting of the entire year. Clouds are on our horizon, too, but we have a lot to do before they usher in the rainy season.

We are caring for the late summer bloomers while at the same time making room for cool-weather annuals to supply fall and winter color. It's shopping time for spring bulbs, and time to plant those that don't require a cooling period. Perennials can be planted now, to bloom next summer. Go to your local nursery and revel in the riches of bedding plants—annual and perennial—available this month.

We usually get a big wind or two at this time of year in Southern California, so don't neglect the precautionary chores of placing potted plants in a sheltered spot where they won't be blown over. Check on plants that need staking to be sure they have ample support in windy weather. Stakes already in place should be checked if they have been in the soil over a long period of time; watering can wash soil away and loosen the stakes. (See **The Art of Staking,** *April.*)

Compost can be a heap of help for the garden. This is the time to start your compost heap, if you have not done so already, in order to take advantage of the wealth of leaves. If you have no deciduous trees (conversational Gardenese for those that shed their leaves), ask your neighbors to let you have some of the leaves from theirs; you'll be amazed at their enthusiastic cooperation, unless, of course, they are composters! (For how and why to compost, see **The Art of Composting,** *September.*)

DO IT NOW

Azaleas and Camellias

Keep the soil constantly moist. This is of prime importance now, while they are setting buds.

Blue Lily Turf

It's time to divide this handsome perennial. Dig the clump out with a spading fork, and pull apart gently into several sections. Replant in thoroughly moistened soil in full sun or partial shade. A handful of bone meal in the planting hole, with some compost, gives a good start for the new divisions. (See *June,* "Let's Get Growing.")

Canna

This is the time to cut back cannas to make way for a new stand of the attractive foliage. Cut them back as close to the ground as possible.

Coleus

If you planted coleus from seed (see *March*), you will have some striking new color combinations that you won't want to lose. Don't leave them to the buffeting of wind and rain, or for the killing breath of the first frost. Pot them and bring them in for the winter. They make wonderful gifts, too. When you dig them, take a generous amount of the soil so the roots won't be unduly disturbed. Make a circle of perhaps 6 inches in diameter and gently lift the plant out. Place it in an 8-inch pot into which you have placed crocks (bits of broken clay pots) and enough potting mix to cushion the plant and its soil. Leave about an inch between the soil surface and the top of the pot to make watering easier and to avoid spillage. Make some cuttings of the more striking colors. Coleus can be propagated from cuttings any time of the year. (See **The Art of Propagation from Softwood Cuttings,** *March.*)

Daylily

Daylilies will profit from a bit of tidying. Snip off or pull out the dead underfoliage; snails like to hide there. If you have some deciduous varieties of daylilies (that is, daylilies that regularly shed their leaves), cut them back now and utilize the space the foliage has been monopolizing by planting cool-weather annuals.

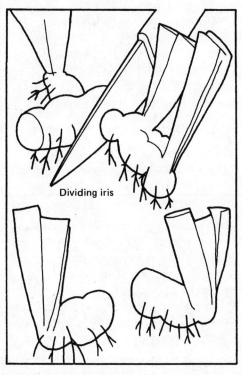

Dividing iris

Iris

Divide bearded iris now if you live in the inland areas. (See *July,* "Do It Now.")

Lily

Stems should be cut back to the base after the flowering period is over. If necessary to divide because of overcrowding, do it when the foliage begins to yellow. Loosen the soil around the clump with a spading fork and gently pry up. Pull apart gently, and replant at once. Some of the bulbs may have stem bulblets—small bulbs clustered along the underground part of the stem. These are little dividends. Detach them gently and replant around the parent plant or in a separate "nursery" bed. Water the newly planted bulbs thoroughly. (See "Lily," *December,* for planting information.)

Tulip

Do your tulip shopping early—not only because this allows you to get the cooling-off period over in time to plant the bulbs in December and January, but because the supply is so abundant now. The longer you delay, the smaller the selection. Right now the bulbs are choice, and the choice is wide— so wide that you may have difficulty choosing wisely if you are just a beginning tulip fancier. The box **The Art of Selecting Tulips** and following chart will help you in regard to color and class.

For planting tulips, see *January,* "Let's Get Growing."

LET'S GET GROWING

Anemone

This easy come, easy grow tuber is just about failureproof, and comes in a variety of forms and colors. Appenina has bright blue, single, daisylike flowers. Blanda has daisylike flowers in pink, blue, and white. Of the poppy-flowered anemones, de Caen is single, in mixed colors; St. Brigid is double or semidouble, in mixed colors.

Ground Rules. Which way is down? A good deal of confusion seems to exist

THE ART OF SELECTING TULIPS

Our mild winters limit the classes that we may choose from. While tulips naturalize (conversational Gardenese for "adapt") in cold winter regions, we must treat them as annuals in Southern California, in most cases, and store them in the refrigerator 6 to 8 weeks in order to provide them with a period of artificial dormancy as a substitute for cold weather. Here are seven classes, and specific names, that do well in our area.

The seven classes may be described as follows:

☐ *Cottage* (also known as Single Late): large, egg-shaped, sometimes elongated flowers.

☐ *Darwin:* large, single-cupped flowers squared off at the base and with a square look to the tops.

☐ *Darwin Hybrid:* largest of the species Tulips, with huge single cups; noted for brilliance of coloring.

☐ *Double Late:* resemble peonies; flowers are large and heavy, double.

☐ *Greigii:* large, long-lasting flowers, cup-shaped, with a wider range of heights, from 4 to 18 inches; marked and mottled foliage.

☐ *Lily Flowered:* pointed, reflexed (folded back) petals, giving them a strong resemblance to lilies.

☐ *Parrot:* large flowers, fringed or scalloped, reminiscent of a parrot's feathers.

The chart does not include the Early, Breeder, Mendel, or Triumph classes, since they will not do well here. (An exception is Garden Party, which is in the Triumph class.)

regarding the way to plant anemones. The American tubers have a definite pointed shape. Plant them point DOWN. The Dutch varieties are flat, rather shapeless. Set them on edge. Plant them in full sun or light shade.

Prepare the soil by working in compost, leaf mold, or peat moss to ensure good drainage. Dig to about a foot, sprinkle bone meal at the bottom—just enough to barely coat the soil—then fill in to about 2 inches from the top; set the tubers in place and cover. Water well at time of planting, then don't water again until the green tips show through the soil. DON'T PRESOAK THE TUBERS. This is very common procedure, but while it may speed up the sprouting process it can cause rot.

As the leaves develop, gradually increase watering, and as buds form, keep the soil moist right through the blooming period.

Daffodil

Daffodils are the best-behaved bulbs in the garden and will naturalize in Southern California, coming into radiant bloom and

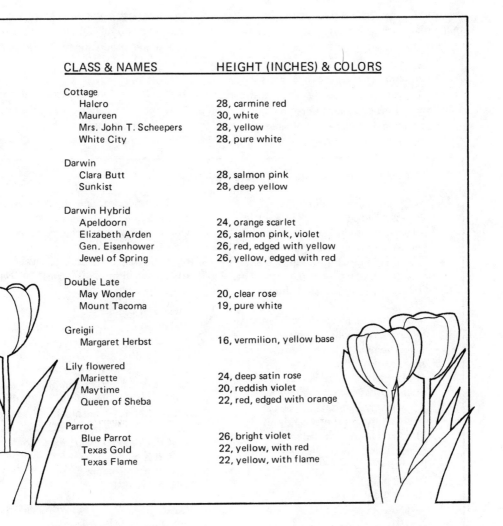

CLASS & NAMES	HEIGHT (INCHES) & COLORS
Cottage	
Halcro	28, carmine red
Maureen	30, white
Mrs. John T. Scheepers	28, yellow
White City	28, pure white
Darwin	
Clara Butt	28, salmon pink
Sunkist	28, deep yellow
Darwin Hybrid	
Apeldoorn	24, orange scarlet
Elizabeth Arden	26, salmon pink, violet
Gen. Eisenhower	26, red, edged with yellow
Jewel of Spring	26, yellow, edged with red
Double Late	
May Wonder	20, clear rose
Mount Tacoma	19, pure white
Greigii	
Margaret Herbst	16, vermilion, yellow base
Lily flowered	
Mariette	24, deep satin rose
Maytime	20, reddish violet
Queen of Sheba	22, red, edged with orange
Parrot	
Blue Parrot	26, bright violet
Texas Gold	22, yellow, with red
Texas Flame	22, yellow, with flame

increasing amiably year after year. They have very few problems and attract no pests.

The only problem you are likely to have is selecting what you want, since there are hundreds of varieties. The best way is to start with a few, then expand your stock.

What's in a name? Maybe a little confusion! *Daffodil narcissus, jonquil*—all are correct, but daffodil is the one most commonly used. Narcissus is the family or botanical name. However, the dainty Cragford, Paper White, Soleil d'Or, and others that produce sprays of flowers are called narcissus.

King Alfred, one of the trumpet daffodils, holds the record for all-time popularity. The blossoms are a perfect golden yellow on long, sturdy stems. It blooms around March. Beersheba, also a trumpet, is white.

If you like a more delicate type of daffodil try the Paper Whites, which bloom as early as December. Soleil d'Or and Cragford bloom soon after.

Try the cyclaminius type, such as Peeping Tom, for February bloom (called cyclaminius because the petals curve back, much like those of the cyclamen).

Flowers of the triandrus varieties are pendulous and fragrant. They bloom in April. Winding up the season, in May, is the Poet's Narcissus, petals usually white, with a shallow, yellow cup edged in red.

When buying daffodil bulbs, always look for those with two points at the top. These are called "double nosed," and are really two-in-one, producing two stalks instead of one.

Tips to Make You Tops with Daffodils
1. In the hot interior valleys, they must have partial shade. In the cooler areas,

---

THE ART OF USING EDGING PLANTS

Get the edge on winter. Well-planned edgings can do a lot to soften and disguise beds that are in a period of dormancy or transition.

Planted in rows outlining a planting area, they can be eye-catchers to draw attention from the rest of the planting space. Even a bed or border that is lying fallow (conversational Gardenese for unplanted) will take on a well-groomed look when ornamented with edging plants.

Many ground covers are effective when used as edging plants. Among them are alyssum saxatile, sweet alyssum, and perennial candytuft (see **The Art of Growing Ground Covers,** *August*), and any of the dwarf bell-flowers. (See *July,* "Let's Get Growing.")

Try these, also:

Linaria
Also called Morocco toadflax and baby snapdragon, this hardy annual is excellent for edging because of its compact growth style. It resembles the snapdragon closely and grows to a height of about 10 inches. The colors are pink, purple, violet, red, and yellow.

Ground Rules. Sow the seeds where they are to grow, in average soil but with plenty of sun. They may take as long as three weeks to germinate, so be patient. When the seedlings have their true leaves, thin to 10 inches. Linaria is another thirsty one.

Pansy and Viola
These are probably the most intriguing and effective of edging plants. Both are of the Viola family. The pansy is the more striking of the two, both as to color combinations and flower size. The violas are daintier, self-colored (all one color) in shades of violet, apricot, yellow, and blue.

If the bedding plants are set out early this month, you will have an abundance of bloom before Thanksgiving.

Tips to Make You Tops with Pansies and Violas
1. The soil should be worked thoroughly, dug to about 12 inches, and pulverized. Work in plenty of organic material such as compost or leaf mold. The location should be a sunny one, except in the hot interior valleys, where the October heat may be too severe.

such as the inner coastal and coastal, give them full sun, although they will do well also in filtered sun.

2. The primary need is for good drainage. Dig the soil to a depth of at least a foot. Add some bone meal 2 or 3 pounds to a 100-square-foot area—and plenty of compost. Do this soil preparation several days before planting; water well, and allow time for the soil to settle.

3. Plant the bulbs 6 to 8 inches deep. (If your soil is on the heavy side, plant them 6 inches deep.)

4. Daffodils tend to work their way down in the ground over a period of several years. This means you must water them

Either delay planting until November, or provide partial shade.

2. Set the plants out in late afternoon, and water thoroughly. It's a good idea to mulch with compost, since these plants are thirsty ones and like to have their roots kept cool.

They should be set just a trifle high so that the soil doesn't settle on the crowns (center of the plant). Two of the few problems are wilt and root rot, both of which are caused by heavy, soggy soil.

3. After the first two weeks, begin a once-a-month feeding of organic fish fertilizer. But don't get it on the foliage, which can be burned by contact.

4. Keep picking the blossoms—they are lovely in bouquets—and remove the faded flowers promptly. They will quickly go to seed otherwise, which means an end to blooming.

5. Rotate your "crop." Planted repeatedly in the same place, pansies have a tendency to develop fungus diseases that infect the soil and create a continuing problem.

6. For edgings, set the plants 8 inches apart; for bedding purposes, 6 to 8 inches apart. A double row is lovely to edge a large bed. Place the pansies (8 to 10 inches in height) behind the lower-growing violas (6 to 8 inches).

7. Using violas only, alternate the pale yellow with blue, or the blue with apricot.

more than some of the close-to-the surface bulbs.

5. They need no special feeding the first year, but in subsequent years, between October and December, sprinkle a light top dressing of bone meal on the bed, just enough to coat the surface.

6. After the flowers have faded, let the foliage brown down (this will take as long as a month) before cutting it back. The bulb is drawing nourishment from this top growth. Continue a regular watering schedule during this period.

Ranunculus

This is another easy come, easy grow bulb. It gets its name from the Latin for "little frog," which is indicative of its meadow origin. (Anemones are of the same family.) The flowers are double and semidouble; the colors are almost unbelievable in their range, including crimson, pink, purple, orange, yellow, scarlet, and white. Heights are from 10 to 14 inches.

Tips to Make You Tops with Ranunculuses

1. When you buy them, select the larger sizes. There is a direct relationship between the size of the bulb (actually a tuber, but classed as a bulb, and let's not get into that!) and the number of flowers it will produce.

2. Generally speaking, ranunculuses want a sunny location, but give them partial shade if you live in the inland areas. The soil should be well-drained, on the light side, which means it's important to add such amendments as compost, leaf mold, or peat moss.

3. The bulbs resemble little claws. Be sure to plant them with the *claws down*—this is where the roots will come from— 1 1/2 or 2 inches deep, 6 inches apart.

4. Water well at time of planting, then withhold water until the first shoots appear. (If the temperature climbs up into the 90s during that period, it might be well to water moderately once or twice.) Once the shoots are up, they must be kept moist right on through the blooming season.

5. If you want them to come up again next year, withhold watering completely after the bloom period ends. If that is impossible, they must be dug up and stored (in any dark, dry place) until next year. The alternative, of course, is to plant them in containers. Or buy new bulbs every year—they are inexpensive.

Sweet Pea, Bush

Want to get away from that struggle with trellis or wire or string supports for sweet pea vines? Are you tired of having to drag out the ladder to get at those choice blossoms way up at the top?

Plant the bush variety now for January bloom. Ferry-Morse has one called Knee-Hi, bushing out into low, spreading mounds of bloom, with the traditional sweet pea colors, on 8- to 10-inch stems with five or six blossoms per stem. Burpee has a bush type called Galaxy.

Ground Rules. Use as you would any other plant for beds or borders. Work in compost to improve the soil structure, and enrich also with bone meal, 2 ounces per yard of row. Water and let it settle overnight.

Sow the seeds an inch deep, 3 to 4 inches apart, in full sun. Thin to 6 inches apart when true leaves appear. (The first set of leaves called "seed leaves," look nothing like the second set, or "true" leaves.)

Because the short runners will try to reach out to a fence or wall, keep the plants a distance of 18 inches from any such surface.

Water frequently after the seeds sprout, and fertilize once a month during bloom season with a low-nitrogen balanced fertilizer such as 2-10-10.

FOUR BEAUTY SPOTS FOR OCTOBER PLANTING

You can be your own landscape designer! Here are four suggested combinations of plants with similar sun, shade, soil, and moisture requirements. These small adventures in color and style are planned to beautify problem areas or to brighten dull sections of the garden. Start with these, then try working out your own designs.

NAME	HEIGHT (INCHES) & SUGGESTED COLORS	SUN/SHADE	SOIL
Bulbs:			
Daffodil: King Alfred	18, golden yellow	Sun (light shade, inland)	Well drained
Dutch Iris: Wedgwood	20-24, deep blue	Sun (light shade, inland)	Well drained
Bedding Plants:			
Pansy	8-10, mixed	Sun	Fertile, moist
Viola	6-8, blue, yellow	Sun	Fertile, moist
Seeds:			
Linum (Scarlet Flax)	18, scarlet	Sun	Average
Stock	18-24, white	Sun	Average
Seeds:			
California Poppy	12, mixed (crimson, rose, yellow, etc.)	Sun	Average
Tidytip	12-18, yellow, tipped with white	Sun	Average

OTHER PLANTABLES FOR OCTOBER

Here are additional plants that may be started this month. The planting information will be found in the chapters indicated below by month. Unless otherwise stated, reference is to "Let's Get Growing" section.

SEEDS

Alyssum Saxatile	*November*	Lobelia	*January* "Beauty Spots"
Baby's Breath	*July*	Mignonette	*January* "Beauty Spots"
Bells-of-Ireland	*June*	Nicotiana	*May* "Beauty Spots"
Calendula	*August, November*	Painted Tongue	*June* "Beauty Spots"
Candytuft, Annual	*April;* also *September* "Beauty Spots"	Petunia	*March*
		Phlox	*May*
Carnation	*January*	Scabiosa	*July* "Beauty Spots"
Chrysanthemum	*March, November*	(Pincushion Flower)	
Clarkia	*September*		
Delphinium	*February*	Schizanthus	*September*
English Daisy	*February* "Beauty Spots"	Snapdragon	*September*
Forget-me-not	*March* "Beauty Spots"	Stock	*August*
Foxglove	*August*	Sweet Alyssum	*August, November*
Gaillardia	*January;* also *February* "Beauty Spots"	Sweet Pea (climbing)	*February*
Godetia	*February* "Beauty Spots"	Verbena	*January;* also *March* and *September* "Beauty Spots"
Hollyhock	*February*	Virginia Stock	*November*
Larkspur	*May* "Beauty Spots"		

BEDDING PLANTS

African Daisy	*November*	Petunia	*March*
Alyssum Saxatile	*November*	Primrose, Fairy	*January*
Calendula	*August, November*	Snapdragon	*September*
Coral Bells	*July*	Stock	*August*
English Daisy	*February* "Beauty Spots"	Sweet Pea (climbing)	*February*
English Primrose	*January*	Sweet William	*January* "Beauty Spots"
Foxglove	*August*	Viola	*September* and *October* "Beauty Spots"
Iceland Poppy	*August*		
Penstemon	*January;* also *April* "Beauty Spots"		

BULBS

Crocus	*January*	Lily	*December*
Freesia	*September*	Sparaxis	*November*
Hyacinth	*January*	Tulip	*January*

November

Plant of the Month: Sparaxis (Wand Flower). The South Africans call it "Harlequin Flower" because of the brightness and the variety of the colors: yellow, white, shades of orange, and dark purple. Plant it now for a glory of bloom in April and May. It's a wonderful cut flower, too.

November

The Thankful Month—
A Time of Lavish Planting

**Clean up, separate, and
plant, plant, plant!**

November gets its name from the Latin word for *nine,* because on the old Roman calendar it was the ninth month (and had 29 days instead of 30). It has been a time of counting our blessings ever since Pilgrim days, although what we think of as the first Thanksgiving, in 1621, was primarily a three-day feast in celebration of the harvest. Thanksgiving took on its true significance the following year. A disastrous drought had burned the gardens brown and shriveled the corn in the fields. When, after a day of prayer, the welcome rains began and a ship arrived with supplies, a day of thanksgiving was proclaimed. It did not become a day of national observance until 1864, when it was so proclaimed by President Lincoln.

Southern California gardeners have plenty to be thankful for in November. It is, believe it or not, one of the most exciting months of

the year, for planting. In terms of seed for winter and spring bloom, we need all the self-control we can muster; there are so many that can be sown directly into the ground now. As for bulbs, we are dazzled by the shape of springs to come. It's a time of lifting and dividing, too—don't grumble at the prospect; we're digging dividends.

It's clean-up time too around the garden, removing leaves (but just as far as the compost heap) and debris that might serve as a winter shelter for snails and other pests. This is a time for cutting back, feeding, and fertilizing.

If you are planning to use pots and other containers for bulbs, they should be thoroughly scrubbed out and made ready for the new tenants. Scrub with an old-fashioned scrubbing brush. Fungus infections can be carried over in bits of soil, and drainage holes can be clogged by old pieces of dried roots. So scrub (using soap and water or just water alone), then rinse and leave in the sun to dry.

Of course it's a lot simpler to do the cleaning of pots when they are first emptied, but not many of us are that disciplined. The impulse is to stack one on top of another in a corner of the tool house or garage until we are suddenly appalled by the numbers of them, recalling English novelist Angela Thirkell's rueful observation about the perils of leaving dirty dishes in the sink: "They marry and have children."

It's time for Santa—but this one brings problems, not gifts. The Santa Ana winds, hot, drying, and capricious, seem to literally suck the moisture from the soil. Be sure to water thoroughly after one of these freak winds.

Don't discontinue regular watering entirely just because we may be getting an occasional rain. How much to water depends on the soil—whether heavy or light—as well as on the moisture needs of various plants. (See **The Art of Watering,** *May.*)

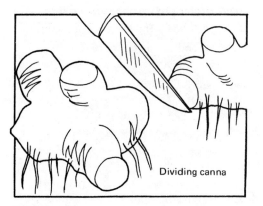

Dividing canna

DO IT NOW

Canna

Cut back cannas so that they stand no higher than 6 inches; close to ground level is even better. They will begin sending up new shoots soon, so make way for the new foliage to dress up the garden

Dahlia

Now is the time to dig those dahlia tubers. The main idea, next to getting them out of the ground, is to get them out in good shape, so be careful not to damage them with the tines of the spading fork or the edge of the spade.

First cut the tops back to about 6 inches. Dig a circle about 12 inches around the plant, then gently pry up the clump. Easy does it—the roots must not be broken.

Shake off the soil and spread the clump of tubers on a flat surface in the sun to dry. But first cut the tops back to 2 inches, and hold the clump upside down for a moment

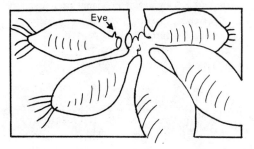

Eye

so that any moisture in the hollow stem will drain off.

Next step: Pack the dried clump of tubers in a box of sand, sawdust, or peat moss (dry), and place the box in a cool, dry place—garage, tool house, or basement—until you have some leisure time to separate the tubers. Or you may prefer to get this job out of the way at the time you dig them.

It's easy—and fun, in a way. With a sharp knife, neatly cut each tuber where it attaches to the parent stem, just above the "eye" or bud. You will be slicing off a bit of the stem with the tuber. (The eye is conversational Gardenese for that lumpy little thing at the point of joining, or slightly above.)

Dust the cut sections with sulfur to avoid any possibility of rotting. Discard the tubers that don't show any indication of a developing eye. Now cover the separated tubers with the storage material (above) and leave them until planting time. (See "Dahlia," *April.*)

Gladiola

Gladiolas should be dug any time after the foliage has yellowed. Loosen the soil and gently pry up the corms. (Technically they are corms, but classed as bulbs. A corm is similar to a bulb, but without scales.)

Cut back the foliage to within half an inch of the top of the corm. Spread the corms in the sun, or in any warm, dry place, to mature. You'll know when they are ready for the next step: The old corm (sometimes called the "mother" corm) at the base of the new one will come away easily. Discard the old corms. Store the new ones in single layers, not on top of each other, in a cool, dry place where the temperature will be approximately 40 to 50 degrees, until January. This provides the important dormant period. Air circulation is important in this storage time, so leave the bags or boxes open. (See "Gladiola," *February,* for planting instructions.)

Vacationing Plants

Remember to bring in any plants you may have plunged for the summer. *Plunging* is conversational Gardenese for the practice of setting a potted plant up to its brim in the garden soil. The pot must be clay in order to draw moisture from the ground through the porous sides. The plant gets a summer vacation, and so do you, since it requires little care and virtually no watering. Another advantage is that when it's time to bring the plant in for the winter, there is no transplanting shock. The pot is simply lifted out, tidied up, and brought indoors.

THE ART OF BULB COVERS

Plan and plant now to make the bulb beds beautiful in those in-between times—before the bulbs are up and blooming, or when they have finished blooming and are in that awkward aftermath, with foliage drying down. Those are the times when you will rejoice over ground covers. But be selective; not all ground covers are suitable for this particular purpose.

Their practical aspects are as important as their beautifying uses. Their shallow roots will not compete with the bulbs for nourishment; they prevent the soil from being washed away before the bulbs are up, and (later on) from being splashed on the blooming bulbs. They also keep down weeds, and—one of their special talents—they prevent the soil from overheating; in other words, they act as living mulches.

Most are available in flats. Some may be started from seed, but the quickest way is to use the bedding plants, if available. Here are just a few to work with:

Alyssum Saxatile. Also called Basket-of-gold, this is the perennial alyssum. Height is 6 to 12 inches, and the masses of minute yellow-gold flowers bloom from spring into summer. It requires little care and will thrive in just about any kind of soil. It wants full sun. BUT it takes time to bring Basket-of-gold into bloom. A nurseryman told me recently that few nurseries will bother to stock the bedding plants because of the long period between seed and bloom (up to 300 days). So you must plant the seeds and be patient. It's worth waiting for, and will be around for a long time.

Candytuft, Perennial. It is probably the most popular of ground covers for bulb beds. It blooms from spring into summer, with the snowiest of white domelike flowers, and the evergreen foliage is attractive all year.

Plant it in full sun or partial shade, but be sure it has well-drained soil. It needs to be well watered. The dwarf variety is ideal for covering bulb beds; the taller (8 to 10 inches) is charming when interplanted with tulips, daffodils, or anemones. Start with bedding plants and propagate from cuttings. (See **The Art of Propagation from Softwood Cuttings,** *March.*)

Creeping Buttercup. Well adapted for use under trees, it likes partial shade. The double, butter-yellow

LET'S GET GROWING

African Daisy, Trailing (Osteospermum)

This is one of those reliable, low-maintenance, ready-when-you-are plants that will grow just about anywhere. It's often planted along freeways, which accounts for its nickname, "freeway daisy."

Set out now, the plants will be well established by late winter or early spring. The flowers are pale lavender with purple centers, but fade to almost white after the first day. Bloom period is from November through March, and the foliage is evergreen.

African daisy is a lavish bloomer, but tends to close its flowers on overcast days. It's ridiculously easy to propagate from

flowers bloom from spring into summer. The foliage is an attractive dark green. The sprawling stems root at the joints, to form a green carpet. Set the bedding plants about 12 inches apart. Excellent as a cooling ground cover for trumpet daffodils. Oddly enough, Creeping Buttercup is classed as a weed when it wanders where it isn't wanted. (See **The Art of Weeding,** *February.*) English Daisy, too, acquires weed status when it establishes itself in lawns—all of which bears out Emerson's sage observation that "a weed is a plant whose virtues have not yet been discovered."

Herniaria. This will grow almost anywhere, in sun or partial shade. It has prostrate stems, about 6 inches long, and attractive foliage with tiny, inconspicuous, greenish-yellow flowers. It makes a solid-looking carpet of green, turning bronze in the winter. (The Greeks gave it the name *herniaria* because it was considered a cure for hernia.) Use the bedding plants.

Potentilla Cinerea (Cinquefoil). Looking like a yellow-flowered strawberry plant, this is beautiful at the base of daylilies. It grows to 6 inches, usually a little less, and adapts to practically any soil. You can plant it in either sun or shade. Use the bedding plants.

Potentilla Verna. This is a little more compact, and better for the hot inland areas because it is heat-resistant and drought-tolerant. Use bedding plants.

Sweet Alyssum (the annual alyssum). It likes sun but will grow in light shade, though the bloom will be sparser. The 4-inch, white Carpet of Snow, is just right for the bulb bed. Cut it back to half its height after the bloom begins to diminish, and you will get another round. (See *August* for planting instructions.) It is available in flats, but grows easily from seed, and will reseed bountifully.

Virginia Stock. An annual that leaps into bloom only six weeks after you sow the seeds, it gives quick color—pink, rose, lavender, white—and a profusion of bloom. The four-petaled blossoms look like miniature stock, although it is not of that family at all. Sow the seeds now where it is to grow, and give it full sun. (But when planted in spring, for summer bloom, it will need partial shade if you live in an inland location.)

cuttings: Just detach a piece at the base of the plant and plant directly into the ground. Thus, if you start with a dozen plants, or with a flat, you can expand the original number without further expense.

Tips to Make You Tops with African Daisies
1. Average soil, on the sandy side, and a sunny location will keep it happy.
2. To plant on a level area, spade the soil to a depth of 12 inches and break up the clods. It never hurts to add compost to get the roots off to a good start, but this sturdy plant will manage without any added attention.
3. It's not for small spaces—it's a sprawler, which adds to its virtues as a ground cover as well as a bedding plant to cover problem areas along driveways and parkings. The branches sprawl out as far as 2 feet or more, and put down roots, binding down the soil and thus discouraging erosion.
4. When planting on a slope (and this is the ideal situation for this plant), don't spade up the area. Dig separate holes for each plant, using a trowel. Then if the rains start before the roots have a good hold, the plants will stay in place—and so will the soil.
5. African daisy is relatively drought-tolerant, and will bloom intermittently almost around the year, but chiefly from November through March. Its evergreen foliage makes it attractive even when it is not in bloom. *Drought-tolerant* doesn't mean you can neglect it, of course. But you don't have to coddle this plant.
6. Its sprawling habit must be taken into consideration in the matter of spacing the plants. Space them at least 18 inches apart. Interplant with sweet alyssum until African daisy can cover the planting area.
7. The plants should be trimmed back once a year, around May or June. Simply snip off the old, shaggy branches. New growth—and more flowers—will replace the old.

Allium, Giant

For something a little different (and that's the only *little* thing about it), plant this distinctively beautiful bulb, a relative of the onion.

Yes, even onions can be beautiful! Take a close look sometime in the vegetable garden at the oddly pretty blossoms of onions gone to seed. Allium is a glamorized onion, with a spectacular 8-inch globe-shaped blossom composed of hundreds of violet-colored florets. The stems get up to 5 feet, with 20-inch leaves that look much like any lily foliage—long, straplike, and growing in basal clusters. If you have the space and the inclination for a unique but easy-to-grow conversation-starter, here it is.

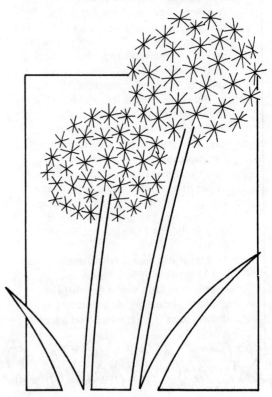

Ground Rules. It has two requirements: full sun and good drainage. Prepare the soil by digging it to a depth of approximately 12 inches and breaking up the clods with a trowel or any other small tool. If the soil is on the heavy side, add compost or peat moss to improve the drainage. Set the bulbs so that the tips are just below the soil surface. It is an ideal patio plant, too. And dried, it is used for flower arrangements or decorative purposes. It blooms in July. When the flower head fades, let it stay on the stem until it is dry, then cut it, with several feet of the stem on it, and hang it upside down in any cool, well-ventilated place to dry further. For decorative use, insert a slender stick, such as the very slim bamboo stakes, or even coathanger wire, into the hollow stem.

Daffodil Garlic is a smaller version, growing to 12 inches. The flower heads are about 3 inches, in white only. This will naturalize in our Southern California gardens, and is also a distinctive cut flower. *(Naturalize* is conversational Gardenese for a plant's adapting to the climate and soil so that it increases without further care.)

Golden Garlic has bright gold flowers borne on 12-inch stems. It's very effective combined with the daffodil garlic for contrast.

Plant any of them near roses, to increase the fragrance of the rose. As to the garlic or onion scent you might expect to encounter with the alliums, the only time it is evident is when the foliage is bruised. The same ground rules apply to all three.

Both of the smaller alliums above are suitable for hillside plantings, under deciduous trees (trees that regularly shed their leaves) and on canyon banks.

Kafir Lily

Also known as Clivia miniata, this plant is available in gallon cans at the nursery, and with very little care you will have it blooming for Christmas, or by January at the latest. It will glorify your garden or patio for three or four months with its brilliant clusters of flame-colored orange or yellow flowers. For more variety in coloring, get the Belgium hybrids, with deep red-orange blossoms, or the Zimmermans, which have white, as well as red, yellow, and orange flowers.

The evergreen foliage is attractive the year round. Clivia or Kafir lily—one name is used as often as the other—can be left in the ground or container for several years without being divided. More good news: It is virtually pest- and problem-free. Mealybugs may appear now and then, but they are easily whisked off with a Q-Tip dipped in rubbing alcohol.

Ground Rules. Kafir lily needs a fairly rich soil, with plenty of humus. Plant it in partial shade—never where it will get direct sun. Never feed it when it is in bloom, but liquid fish or any good, balanced fertilizer should be used a couple of times a year. (See **The Art of Fertilizing,** *March.*) Be stingy with water at blossom time.

Shirley Poppy

This plant is long on bloom and short on care. Plant it this month and it will flower profusely from spring throughout the summer and on into September. The double or single blossoms, with silky, papery petals, are over 2 inches across and come in colors of pink, red, salmon, orange, and white. Some are bicolored.

They make delightful cut flowers. Wait until the buds are just showing color, then cut. Char the ends of the stems with a match or a candle flame, to promote longevity in water.

Ground Rules. Sow the seeds in practically any soil as long as drainage is good and there is an abundance of sun. It doesn't require feeding and likes a rather dry soil; water a couple of times a week in hot weather, once a week in moderate weather. Don't water overhead because of the delicate texture of the petals. To ensure a long period of bloom, remove seed pods as soon as they appear.

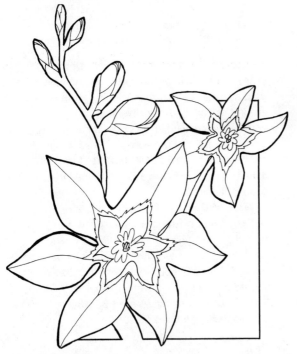

Sparaxis

Also called Wand Flower, this is one of the easiest bulbs (corms) to grow; it's

surprising that sparaxis is not used more lavishly than it is. The colors are bright and varied, in solids, bicolors, and tricolors. The range takes in yellow, white and yellow, dark purple, and many shades of orange and red. Plant it now for lavish bloom in April and May.

Tips to Make You Tops with Sparaxis

1. Plant it where it will get lots of sun; that's the only thing it is particular about.
2. The soil can be average, but like any bulb, it needs good drainage. Spade the bed to about 12 inches, pulverize the soil, and work in some compost or peat moss.
3. Set the little corms 3 inches deep, 3 or 4 inches apart.

4. Water moderately. Unlike many bulbs or corms, it can do with very little moisture. But that doesn't mean it should be allowed to dry out.
5. It multiplies rapidly, so take that into consideration in planting it. When it finishes blooming, let the foliage dry down; the corms will be drawing nourishment from the foliage for next year's bloom. Cut back only after this drying down period is over.
6. Don't discontinue watering during the "drying down" period. A 1-inch layer of compost mulch will help retain moisture.

FOUR BEAUTY SPOTS FOR NOVEMBER PLANTING

You can be your own landscape designer! Here are four combinations of plants with similar sun, shade, soil, and moisture needs. These small adventures in color and style are designed to beautify problem areas or to brighten dull sections of the garden. Start with some of these, then try working out your own designs.

NAME	HEIGHT (INCHES) & SUGGESTED COLORS	SUN/SHADE	SOIL
Bulbs:			
Cyclamen	10, white	Semishade	Loamy, well drained
Kafir Lily	18, orange	Semishade	Loamy, well drained
Bulbs:			
Mariette Tulip	24, deep rose	Sun, light shade	Well drained
White Triumphator	26, white	Sun, light shade	Well drained
Seeds:			
California Poppy, Ballerina Yellow	12, yellow	Sun	Average
Shirley Poppy	24-36, red, white	Sun	Average
Bulbs:			
Anemone—Monarch de Caen	12-14, mixed	Sun, light shade	Well drained
Daffodil—February Gold	6, yellow with orange	Sun, light shade	Well drained
Ipheon—Blue Dicks	12-24, blue	Sun or shade	Any

OTHER PLANTABLES FOR NOVEMBER

Here are additional plants that may be started this month. The planting information will be found in the chapters indicated below by month. Unless otherwise shown, reference is to "Let's Get Growing" section.

SEEDS

Baby's Breath	*July;* also *April* "Beauty Spots"	Linaria	*October*
		Linum	*October* "Beauty Spots"
Bells-of-Ireland	*June*	Lobelia	*January* "Beauty Spots"
Calendula	*August;* also *January* "Beauty Spots"	Mignonette	*January* "Beauty Spots"
		Painted Tongue	*June* "Beauty Spots"
California Poppy	*September;* also *October* "Beauty Spots"	Pansy	*October*
Candytuft, annual	*April;* also *September* "Beauty Spots"	Petunia	*March;* also *April* "Beauty Spots"
Carnation	*January*	Phlox	*May*
Cineraria	*January*	Scabiosa	*May* "Beauty Spots"
Clarkia	*September*	Schizanthus	*September* "Beauty Spots"
Columbine	*February* "Beauty Spots"	Shasta Daisy	*May, August*
Delphinium	*February, April, July*	Snapdragon	*September*
English Daisy	*February* "Beauty Spots"	Stock	*July, August*
Forget-me-not	*March* "Beauty Spots"	Strawflower	*August* "Beauty Spots"
Foxglove	*August*	Sweet Pea (bush)	*October*
Gaillardia	*January;* also *July* "Beauty Spots"	Verbena	*January;* also *March* "Beauty Spots"
Godetia	*February* "Beauty Spots"	Viola	*October*
Hollyhock	*February*	Virginia Stock	*October* "Beauty Spots"
Larkspur	*May* "Beauty Spots"	Wild Flowers	*September*

BEDDING PLANTS

Calendula	*August;* also *January* "Beauty Spots"	Pansy	*October*
		Penstemon	*January;* also *April* "Beauty Spots"
Columbine	*February* "Beauty Spots"	Petunia	*March;* also *April* "Beauty Spots"
Coral Bells	*July, September*		
English Daisy	*February* "Beauty Spots"	Snapdragon	*September*
English Primrose	*January;* also *September* "Beauty Spots"	Stock	*August*
Fairy Primrose	*September* "Beauty Spots"	Sweet Pea (bush)	*October*
		Viola	*October*
Foxglove	*August*		
Iceland Poppy	*August*		

BULBS

Anemone	*October*	Kafir Lily	*November*
Babiana	*December*	Lily	*December*
Daffodil	*October*	Ranunculus	*October*
Dutch Iris	*October* "Beauty Spots"	Sparaxis	*November*
Freesia	*September*		

December

Plant of the Month: Lily. It's been around for some 3,000 years, and no wonder! Here's a plant with an incredible color range, including vermilion, silver, gold, tangerine, and yellow spotted with maroon. Planned for progressive blooming, it will glorify the garden from spring to fall. An elegant cut flower, too!

December

A Little Stardust Caught

**Plan a little, plant a little,
give a lot.**

"The true harvest of my daily life," wrote Thoreau, in assessing his Walden experiences, "is somewhat as intangible and indescribable as the tints of morning and evening. It is a little stardust caught, a segment of the rainbow which I have clutched."

Certainly our true harvest as gardeners is more than buds and bulbs and packets of seed. Probably the biggest dividend is a growing sense of creativity, of participating in a never-ending cycle. The year is a clock, with months on the dial, instead of hours. If, in this past year of gardening, we have had some startling successes, we can plan for more expansive achievements. If some of our results were less than thrilling, the ground holds no grudges; we can wind up the clock of the year and start over again! Somewhere along the way we have caught our own bit of stardust and clutched at least a wisp of rainbow.

December, once the tenth month of the year, until Julius Caesar reorganized the calendar, was named prosaically for *decem*, the Latin word for "ten." There is still time to plant bulbs, and there is a sizable list of seeds and bedding plants, but many of us are so caught up in Christmas and holiday activities that we are likely to be more concerned with plans than with plants, with giving than with gardening.

Happily, choosing a gift is no problem for most garden enthusiasts. But if, like Scrooge (though in a different sense), you are haunted by the ghost of the Christmas present, try some of these:

Rainwater, rich in nitrogen, is a fun gift and a welcome one, for friends with house plants. The first good rain is your bargain day! Set a good-sized container under the down spout, or just put several pots or pans around the yard to catch the golden goodies. Then "package" your gift in fancy jars and bottles, wrapped and tied with holiday trimmings. Add a watering pot or a misting sprayer, for good measure.

Flats of bedding plants or the more advanced plants in 4-inch pots make long-lasting gifts. Try delphiniums, chrysanthemums, primroses, and Iceland poppies, for starters.

Books on gardening make good reading for those rainy evenings that are either here or on the way.

Dried flowers, those you raised and dried, are ready now to be made into charming bouquets or flower arrangements. See Bells-of-Ireland, *June;* Baby's Breath, *July;* Straw-flower, *August* "Beauty Spots."

Bulbs can light up the eyes of any gardening buff, especially if you come up with some name varieties your friends or family don't have. (See **The Art of Selecting Tulips,** *October;* "Daffodil," *October;* "Lily," this chapter.)

Tools include everything from small tools such as trowels and hand cultivators to spading forks and wheelbarrows.

Add some glow to the glory of Christmas and the holidays. Just because the nights are too chilly for outdoor entertaining, don't overlook the potential of the garden and patio as part of the decorative scheme.

Edge the path, outline the patio, or light up special corners of the garden with *luminarias.* These are traditional Christmas lights used in many parts of New Mexico, where the custom originated as a method of lighting the way for early-morning churchgoers.

THE ART OF TOOL CARE

Take care of the tools that take care of your garden. Don't leave them out to rust in the rain or to disappear under drifts of leaves.

Put them away clean. Get rid of those little bits of dried dirt; wipe off the grass stains. If you want them to look and be sharp, you'll need something more than elbow grease.

There are several products on the market for cleaning and oiling tools. Most are rust-resisters as well as lubricants. Oil the movable parts, and wipe off blades with a little oil on a soft rag.

When tools need sharpening it's best to take them to a lawnmower shop. Some garden centers and hardware stores have this service also.

Small tools such as trowels and weed diggers should be put away in boxes or drawers where they are readily available for use at odd times during the winter.

Don't put away all hoses, but be sure to drain those that are going into retirement for the winter.

The soaker-sprinklers that have lain under the hedges and in the borders all summer and fall should be wiped clean and drained, coiled loosely, and hung up. (Metal hose racks are inexpensive and will pay for themselves by extending the life of a hose.)

Invest in some hooks and holders for tools. The "gripper clips" are practical and cost less than a packet of seeds.

Hose nozzles should be stored in boxes or drawers.

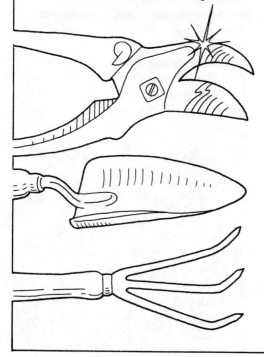

All you need are those squat little vigil or votive candles, brown paper bags, and sand. Most grocery and hardware stores have the candles. Save your small or medium-sized grocery sacks or buy them in packs at the supermarket. Use builder's sand or bird gravel from the pet store. Fill the sack half full. Anchor the candle firmly in the sand. Roll the sack down until it stands about 7 inches high. Light the candle and let 'er glow!

The paper bag acts as a windbreak, much like an old-fashioned lamp chimney, and the flame, seen through the paper, gives a warm and cheerful glow.

If you have a pool and camellias, float the blossoms on the surface of the pool, just before the guests arrive, and set luminarias at intervals around the pool edge.

DO IT NOW

Plants that are dormant now (such as ferns, fuchsias, begonias) will not need fertilizing until early spring. The winter-blooming bedding plants such as calendulas, pansies, primroses, snapdragons, and stock will benefit from a high-nitrogen fertilizer, because the bacteria that usually provide nitrogen in the soil are dormant now.

Agapanthus (Lily-of-the-Nile)

This can be divided now. It is not necessary—or even desirable—to dig up the whole clump, since dividing this stay-at-home plant will slow it down a bit. What looks like one clump is actually a group of clumps. Slide the spade or trowel down into the foliage and take out just the clump or segment you want to move. (Cutting the foliage back to 3 inches from the base will make the whole operation easier. It will grow in again in about a month.) Fill in with soil, and water well, so that the remaining plants won't be left exposed at the roots. Replant the newly dug segment at once. (See *June.*)

Camellias and Azaleas

Don't fail to keep their roots moist if rains are infrequent. Mulching with compost or peat moss will help to keep the roots from drying out. (See **The Art of Mulching,** *February,* and **The Art of Composting,** *September.*)

Chrysanthemum

As soon as the flowers fade, cut the plants back to about 6 inches from the ground.

LET'S GET GROWING

Baboon Flower (Babiana)

Where did a good-looking plant like this one get a name like baboon flower? Not from the hairy leaves, as you might think, but because, in its native Africa, the corms are said to be a favorite food of baboons. (A corm is similar to a bulb, but without scales.)

It's a spring bloomer, belonging to the Iris family. The slightly twisted stems bear flowers in clusters.

Babiana stricta has red flowers and grows to between 8 and 12 inches.

Rubro cyanea has blue flowers with red throats, and *sulphurea* has yellow and white blossoms.

There is a dwarf form, *Babiana plicata,* under 6 inches, with lavender and cream flowers.

Ground Rules. Plant the corms 3 inches deep, 3 inches apart, in full sun. They want light but rather loamy soil. Keep moist, but not to the point of sogginess.

Bird of Paradise (Strelitzia)

This is the official flower of the City of Los Angeles. One look at the exotic blossom tells you how it got its name—the resemblance to a tropical bird is uncanny. The vivid blue and orange flowers with just a touch of white rise on sturdy stems as high as 5 feet, from foliage resembling miniature banana leaves.

It is so large and dramatic looking that it overpowers other plants, so give it a corner to itself, or set plants in rows—a good 5 feet apart. The flowers are striking in indoor arrangements. (Don't confuse it with the tree; this is Strelitzia *reginae.*)

Ground Rules. Full sun in coastal and inner coastal areas, light shade inland. It needs a fertile, well-drained soil. Get the plants in gallon cans. Add compost or peat moss to the planting hole, and about a tablespoon of bone meal. Mulch with a combination of steer manure and compost around the year. Feed spring and fall with organic fish fertilizer. Deep-water twice a week in dry weather, but never water the blossoms directly.

Protect from frost with plastic or newspaper covering when necessary.

Canterbury Bell

The most glamorous and diverse member of the Campanula or Bellflower family, this well-loved hardy biennial comes in several colors (violet blue, lavender, pink, and white) as well as in some intriguing forms. One is called cup-and-saucer, which describes the shape of the flower. One is hose-in-hose (conversational Gardenese for one tubular flower set into another) and others are urn-shaped or bell-shaped. Grown from seed, Canterbury bell won't bloom in its first season, so get the nursery-started bedding plants, available this month, for spring and summer bloom. (See **The Art of Starting from Seeds and Bedding Plants,** *January.*)

Ground Rules. Moist, rich, loamy soil is what it wants, in partial shade. Work in plenty of compost or leaf mold if your soil is on the heavy side. Space the plants 18 inches apart. This is a leafy plant with sizable leaves at the base as well as on the stems. The spikes, on which the clusters of flowers are borne, rise as high as 4 feet. It's a charming cut flower, too. Set the plants a trifle high,

so that soil won't wash over into the basal foliage or be splashed on it in a heavy rain.

Lily

Think big, think lilies! What's so great about them? They stay where you put them; there's no lifting and replanting for at least three or four years. They are incredibly versatile as to color, form, height, and usage. They are as happy in a movable container as in the garden. They make great cut flowers, and many are delightfully fragrant. What's more, they are sociable; they like to mix in with perennials, annuals, or evergreen shrubs.

Don't confuse lilies with such nonlilies as calla lilies, daylilies, or lily-of-the-Nile, which more or less have the title by courtesy. True lilies, LILY lilies, are a separate genus, *Lilium,* having six anthers, three sepals, and three petals (which look like six petals). So if you have been thinking of your callas or agapanthuses or gloriosa lilies as one of the family, don't trot them over to the North American Lily Society's show. (If there's any question, the lilies have the anthers.)

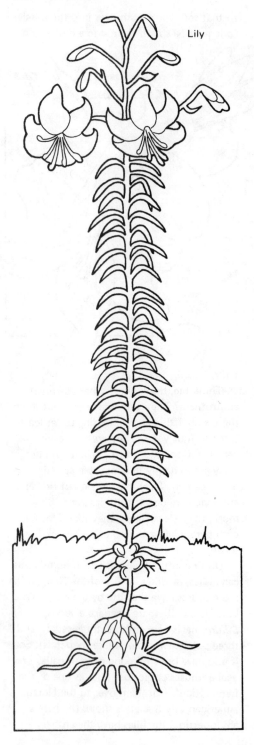

Lily

Lilies were wild flowers originally, and because they didn't always take hold well when suddenly uprooted from their native setting and planted in a different climate and soil, they got the reputation of being as delicate as a Victorian lady with the vapors. But today's hybrids—and most lilies available now are hybrids—are bred for vigor, disease resistance, floriferousness (conversational Gardenese for abundance of bloom), and the floral equivalent of gumption. When you stop to think about it, any plant that can grow as high as 7 feet and bear flowers as much as 8 inches in width, with as many as 30 buds per plant, somehow loses its air of fragility.

As to color, although the poets have tended to limit them to white ("Lily-like, white as snow . . ."), these bulbs can make the garden glow with just about every color in the horticultural paint box—including green. (See *Green Magic* in the list of lilies below.)

Tips to Make You Tops with Lilies

1. The primary requirement for lily culture is well-drained soil. Add plenty of organic matter such as compost, leaf mold, or peat moss. A good basic planting mixture for lilies is one part soil, one part sand, two parts organic matter.

2. Lilies are never dormant, so don't leave the bulbs lying around once you bring them home. If you must delay planting, leave them in the plastic wrappers they come in, or place them in a box of moist peat moss.

3. Select a location that provides at least half a day of sun, with some shade. (The latter is especially important in the inland areas.)

4. If your soil is on the heavy side, plant on a slope or in a raised bed to facilitate good drainage. *(Raised bed* is conversational Gardenese for the

practice of mounding good soil on top of the basic soil. This may be top soil from another section of the garden, or a mixture of soil, compost, and sand, heaped into a mound. Stones or bricks around the raised bed will keep the soil from washing away.)

5. If you are preparing a planting space rather than making a raised bed, spade the soil to a depth of at least 12 inches, preferably 18. Pulverize it and add the organic materials. Don't add manure to the planting holes; it can burn the bulbs. It's all right to use it as a top dressing, spread over the bed after the bulbs are planted.

6. A half cup of bone meal per bulb, at the bottom of the planting hole, will give the roots a good start. For a larger area, figure on 1 pound of bone meal per 20 square feet.

7. Water the bed thoroughly and let it settle for a day or two.

8. Depth of planting depends on size of the bulbs: For most bulbs, 3 to 4 inches of soil is sufficient (figuring from the tip of the bulb); slightly less for small bulbs, more for larger ones. Jumbo bulbs, measuring 9 or 10 inches in circumference, should be planted 6 inches deep. The exception is the Madonna lily: no more than an inch of soil over the tip.

9. Spacing is almost as important as depth: Space small bulbs 6 to 8 inches apart; larger ones, 8 to 12 inches. Jumbos need a minimum of 12 inches, or as much as 16.

10. Cover the bulbs gently, taking care not to damage any sprouts (these may be showing on bulbs for spring planting.) Water in, *thoroughly.*

11. Lilies must be kept constantly moist. The soaker-sprinkler is a good watering tool to use. (See **Easier Ways to Water,** *June.*) Deep-water to a depth of 6 inches at least once a week. A shallow-rooted ground cover will act as a living mulch and keep moisture from evaporating rapidly in hot weather. (See **The Art of Bulb Covers,** *November.*) Never water lilies overhead, always at the base.

12. Keep faded flowers picked off. When cutting the flowers for the house, don't cut the stems any longer than necessary, since the bulbs draw nourishment from stems and foliage for next year's flower production.

13. The stalks should not be cut back until they have yellowed, well after the blooming period is over. But it is important to cut them back then. Don't throw them on the compost heap, but in the trash, in case they are harboring pests or disease.

14. Be sure to keep up a regular watering schedule while the stalks are in the process of yellowing, after the bloom period. The amount of water can be reduced, however. (See **The Art of Watering,** *May.*)

15. Feed lilies after the shoots are up in the spring. Most growers recommend a 5-10-5 fertilizer. (See **The Art of Fertilizing,** *March.*)

16. Lilies can be left to their own devices for several years, growing happily in the same spot. But when the stems become crowded while at the same time getting small and spindly, it's time for a move. (See *October.*)

The only difficult thing about lilies is choosing from among the bewildering varieties, colors, and sizes. Because some types are better suited to Southern California than others, I asked Thomas R. Holmes of Davids & Royston Bulb Company in Gardena to make some suggestions. The box lists 25 varieties from grower Jan de Graaff's Oregon Bulb Farms.

TWENTY-FIVE LILIES FOR SOUTHERN CALIFORNIA GARDENS

NAME AND BLOOM PERIOD	HEIGHT (FEET) AND COLORS
Amber Gold, Late June, early July	4-5, buttercup yellow, maroon spots
Bittersweet, July	to 5, bright orange, black spots
Black Dragon, July	5-6, white with reverse maroon
Burgundy, July	4-5, cherry red to burgundy
Cinnabar, June	2-3, deep red
Crimson Beauty, August	4-6, white, red band
Enchantment, June-July	3-plus, nasturtium red
Golden Splendor, July	5-6, deep golden yellow
Green Magic, July	4-6, white, tinted green
Imperial Crimson, August	5-7, crimson
Imperial Gold, August	5-6, white, gold-striped, maroon spots
Imperial Silver, August	5-6, white, dotted with vermilion
Jamboree, August-September	5-6, crimson tones, silver margin
Joan Evans, Late June, early July	3-4, golden yellow, spotted with maroon
Magic Pink, Early July	2-3, shell pink
Mid-Century Hybrids June-July	3-4, mixed reds, oranges, yellows
Oriental Hybrids Mix, August	4-6, white, pink, crimson, gold bands
Pink Glory, Late July, early August	5-6, shades of pink
Pink Perfection, July	5-6, deep pink
Pirate, July	to 4, tangerine red
Prosperity, Late June, early July	to 3, bright yellow
Rainbow Hybrids, Late May, early June	3-4, golden yellow, orange, mahogany red, bicolors
Red Flare, June-July	3-4, light to dark red
Regale, Late June, early July	3-4, white, yellow throat, dark reverse
White Champion, Spec. September	4-6, white

FOUR BEAUTY SPOTS FOR DECEMBER PLANTING

You can be your own landscape designer! Here are four plant combinations with similar sun, shade, soil, and moisture needs. These small adventures in color and style are designed to beautify problem areas or brighten dull sections of the garden. Start with these; then try working out some of your own designs.

NAME	HEIGHT (INCHES) & SUGGESTED COLORS	SUN/SHADE	SOIL
Bulbs:			
Anemone, Poppy-flowered	12, white	Sun	Well drained
Ranunculus	12-18, mixed	Sun	Well drained
(Plant Anemones 2 inches deep, points down. Ranunculus 2 inches deep, claws down.)			
Bulbs:			
Daffodil (Fortune)	24, yellow with orange	Filtered sun	Well drained
Scilla (Siberian Squill)	6-8, blue	Filtered sun	Well drained
(Plant Daffodils 6 1/2 inches deep; Scilla 3 inches.)			
Bulbs:			
Ornithogalum Star of Bethlehem	6-12, white with green tips	Sun	Average
Sparaxis	9-12, mixed	Sun	Average
(Plant Ornithogalum 3-4 inches deep; Sparaxis 3 inches.)			
Bulbs:			
Daffodil, Francisca Drake	16, white with yellow	Filtered sun	Well drained
Seeds:			
Baby Blue Eyes	8, blue with white centers	Filtered sun	Any

OTHER PLANTABLES FOR DECEMBER

Here are additional plants that may be started this month. The planting information will be found in the chapters indicated below by month. Unless otherwise shown, reference is to "Let's Get Growing" section.

SEEDS

African Daisy	*November*	Hollyhock	*February*
Ageratum	*April;* also *March* "Beauty Spots"	Larkspur	*May* "Beauty Spots"
		Linum	*October* "Beauty Spots"
Baby's Breath	*July*	Mignonette	*January* "Beauty Spots"
Basket-of-gold	*November*	Nemophile (Baby Blue Eyes)	*September*
Bells-of-Ireland	*June*		
Calendula	*August, November*	Painted Tongue	*June* "Beauty Spots"
California Poppy	*September;* also *October* "Beauty Spots"	Pansy	*October*
		Phlox	*May*
Candytuft	*April;* also *September* "Beauty Spots"	Scabiosa	*May* and *July* "Beauty Spots"
Chrysanthemum	*May, June, July, March*	Schizanthus	*September* "Beauty Spots"
Clarkia	*September*	Shasta Daisy	*May*
Columbine	*February* "Beauty Spots"	Stock	*August*
Coreopsis	*May* "Beauty Spots"	Sweet Alyssum	*August, November*
Delphinium	*February*	Sweet Pea	*October, February*
Forget-me-not	*March* "Beauty Spots"	Virginia Stock	*November*
Gaillardia	*January*	Wild Flowers	*September*
Godetia	*February* "Beauty Spots"		

BEDDING PLANTS

African Daisy	*November*	Pansy	*October;* also *March* "Beauty Spots"
Calendula	*August, November*		
Cineraria	*January*	Penstemon	*January;* also *April* "Beauty Spots"
Columbine	*February* "Beauty Spots"	Petunia	*March*
Coral Bells	*July*	Snapdragon	*September*
Delphinium	*February*	Stock	*August*
English Daisy	*February* "Beauty Spots"	Sweet Alyssum	*August, November*
English Primrose	*January*	Sweet Pea	*February* and *October*
Foxglove	*August*	Viola	*October*
Iberis	*May, November*		
Iceland Poppy	*August*		

BULBS

Allium	*November*	Iris, Dutch	*October* "Beauty Spots"
Anemone	*October*	Lily of the Valley	*February*
Cyclamen	*November* "Beauty Spots"	Ranunculus	*October*
Daffodil	*October*	Sparaxis	*November*
Freesia	*September*		

Glossary

Accent Plant: One used to point up or accent a particular setting. Accent plants are usually of a well-defined form, e.g., conical, as in some types of evergreens, or with variegated or distinctive foliage.

Annual: A plant that completes its life cycle in a single season.

Axil: The angle between branch or leaf and the stem from which it grows.

Amendment: Organic material added to the soil to improve the structure, contribute nutrients, etc.

Bedding Plants: Rooted plants already in leaf, sometimes in bloom, ready to be set out.

Biennial: A plant that completes its life cycle in two seasons.

Bloom Fertilizer: One that is low in nitrogen content, but high in phosphorus and potassium, to encourage bloom rather than foliage.

Botanicals: Pesticides derived from plants.

Broadcasting: Sowing seeds by scattering them loosely over the surface of the soil or planting medium, rather than planting in rows.

Bulb Covers: The use of shallow-rooted plants in a bulb bed, to keep the ground cool and to beautify the planting area during the time when the bulbs are not in bloom, or when they have completed their blooming period and the foliage is in process of drying down.

Bulb Pan: A pot about half the depth of the standard flower pot. Used for shallow-rooted plants, bulbs, and seedlings.

Bud Union: The point at which a bud or cutting *(cion)* is united with a rooted stock to produce an improved variety. E.g., on a rose, it is that area at the base of the main stem where the cion has been grafted onto the stem.

Cane: The stem of a woody or herbaceous plant such as the rose. Basal canes are those growing at the base of the plant.

Cion: (Also *scion.*) The detached shoot of a plant used in grafting.

Competitive: Vying for soil nutrients, sun, moisture, etc. Plants that are aggressive in seeking out nourishment at the expense of other plants in the same general area are called "competitive."

Complete Fertilizer: One that contains all three of the principle plant nutrients—nitrogen, phosphorus, and potassium.

Corm: Similar to a bulb, but without scales. Round and rather flat. *Cormels* are young shoots that rise from the base of the corm.

Crossing: The artificial transfer of pollen from one flower to another, to produce hybrids.

Crown: The portion of a plant between root and stem; usually at or close to the soil surface.

Cutting: A piece cut or removed from a plant for propagation purposes.

Deciduous: Plants that shed their leaves in the fall are deciduous. Technically it refers to the dropping of foliage, fruits and petals, but the term is more generally used in reference to foliage.

Deep Watering: The practice of applying water slowly, in sufficient volume to moisten the soil well below the surface.

Damping-off: A fungus disease that causes young seedlings to rot suddenly at the surface level of the soil.

Dormant: Botanically it refers to the period when a plant is not actively growing. Also used with reference to soil bacteria, considered dormant in winter when not releasing nutrients to the soil.

Drainage: The water-holding propensity of soil. Well-drained soil holds moisture in sufficient quantity to sustain a plant's roots, yet is loose-textured enough to let excess moisture drain off.

Drip Line: The perimeter of a plant's spread, where moisture drips from the end of the branches.

Earth Up: To heap soil at the base of large, top-heavy plants in order to anchor them more firmly.

Erosion: Loss of soil through rains or heavy watering. Also called "runoff."

Eye: A bud on a tuber or tuberous root, or a bud on a cutting. Also the contrasting center of a flower, such as the white "eye" of the blue forget-me-not.

Foliage Plant: A plant used primarily for its attractive leaves, such as ferns, begonias and coleuses, etc.

Foliar Feeding: To feed plants by spraying or dusting the foliage, which absorbs the nutrients.

Friable: Crumbly, pulverized, easily worked.

Floriferous: Flowering abundantly.

Ground Cover: A planting of low-growing, usually shallow-rooted plants, for various purposes such as prevention of erosion, etc.

Hose-in-Hose: A flower form wherein one tubular blossom is set within another.

Humus: Decomposed or decomposing animal or vegetable matter forming the organic content of soil.

Hybrid: The result of cross-fertilizing two plants of the same or differing varieties, to produce a superior variety.

Lateral: A branch or cane borne at the side of a plant's main stem.

Leach: To wash away or flush out pollutants or deposits by heavy watering, carrying them in solution to depths below the root zones. Leaching is also used in the context of washing away soil nutrients by excessive amounts of water.

Loam, Loamy: In its general meaning, a rather light-textured fertile soil, rich in humus.

Mulch: A layer of material such as leaf mold, compost, etc. applied to the soil surface around a plant. ("Green Mulch" is used with reference to some ground cover plants that serve the purpose of keeping the soil around a moisture-loving plant cool and moist.)

Naturalize: The process by which a plant will adapt itself to an environment to which it is not native.

Nymph: The immature stage of certain insects.

Perennial: A plant that lasts through at least two seasons, but usually through several or many years.

Picotee: The coloring pattern of certain blossoms having petals edged with a color differing from that of the rest of the petal.

Pinching Back: The practice of removing surplus buds or shoots in order to increase bloom or control the shape of the plant. Also called "Disbudding" or "Disshooting."

Planting Mix: Coarse organic material used primarily for planting shrubs and bare-root plants. It is mixed with the soil to improve the structure.

Plunging: Setting a container in which a plant is growing, into the ground, up to its rim.

Potting Mix: A combination of various components such as sand, loam, leaf mold, etc. The combinations may vary for specific uses, but the packaged commercial potting mix is a rather fine-grained medium suitable for potting plants and starting seeds.

Pricking Out: An intermediate step between planting and transplanting, whereby seedlings are "pricked out" of the flat or container and transferred to another flat until they are large enough and sturdy enough for transplanting in the ground.

Progression: The practice of planting at intervals, to ensure a progression of bloom, rather than having all of the plants in bloom at approximately the same time.

Propagation: The increase of plants, specifically, new plants from existing ones.

Rhizome: A rootstock. While it looks like a root, it is actually an underground stem with roots for gathering nourishment, and with eyes or buds for new growth.

Rosarian: A rose expert or cultivator.

Rotation: The practice of planning and planting so that the same crop does not occupy an area continuously.

Seed Leaves: The first pair of leaves produced by a sprouting seed.

Seedling: A young plant grown from seed.

Sucker: A secondary shoot rising from the lower part of a plant, or from the ground at the base of the plant.

Terminal: End growth. Terminal clusters are clusters of flowers borne at the end of the stem or branch, rather than in the leaf axil.

Thinning: The practice of removing a number of seedlings in order to allow sufficient growing space, nutrients, etc. for those remaining.

Tilth: The condition or workability of soil.

Top Dressing: Material such as manure, bone meal, fertilizer or compost, spread on the surface around a plant and raked into the ground, to supply nutrients. Differs from mulching in that it has only one basic purpose: to supply nutrients; whereas a mulch conserves moisture, protects the plant roots from heat or cold, discourages weeds, and supplies a certain amount of nutrients as well.

Index

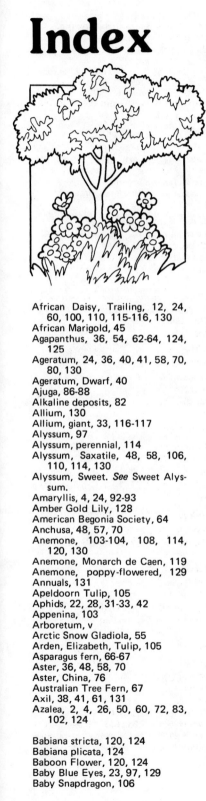

African Daisy, Trailing, 12, 24, 60, 100, 110, 115-116, 130
African Marigold, 45
Agapanthus, 36, 54, 62-64, 124, 125
Ageratum, 24, 36, 40, 41, 58, 70, 80, 130
Ageratum, Dwarf, 40
Ajuga, 86-88
Alkaline deposits, 82
Allium, 130
Allium, giant, 33, 116-117
Alyssum, 97
Alyssum, perennial, 114
Alyssum, Saxatile, 48, 58, 106, 110, 114, 130
Alyssum, Sweet. *See* Sweet Alyssum.
Amaryllis, 4, 24, 92-93
Amber Gold Lily, 128
American Begonia Society, 64
Anchusa, 48, 57, 70
Anemone, 103-104, 108, 114, 120, 130
Anemone, Monarch de Caen, 119
Anemone, poppy-flowered, 129
Annuals, 131
Apeldoorn Tulip, 105
Appenina, 103
Arboretum, v
Arctic Snow Gladiola, 55
Arden, Elizabeth, Tulip, 105
Asparagus fern, 66-67
Aster, 36, 48, 58, 70
Aster, China, 76
Australian Tree Fern, 67
Axil, 38, 41, 61, 131
Azalea, 2, 4, 26, 50, 60, 72, 83, 102, 124

Babiana stricta, 120, 124
Babiana plicata, 124
Baboon Flower, 120, 124
Baby Blue Eyes, 23, 97, 129
Baby Snapdragon, 106

Baby's Breath, annual, 24, 70, 76, 90, 100, 110, 120, 122, 130
Baby's Tears, 88-89
Bare root stock, 20
Basal cane, 3, 131
Basal stem, 51
Basket-of-Gold. *See* Alyssum Saxatile.
Bearded Iris, 60-61, 74, 93, 103
Beauty spots, 11, 23, 35, 47, 57, 69, 79, 89, 99, 109, 119, 129
Bedding plants, 2, 8, 10, 12, 24, 35, 36, 38, 47, 48, 57, 58, 69, 70, 72, 79, 80, 89, 90, 99, 100, 102, 109, 110, 114-115, 120, 122, 125, 130, 131
Beersheba daffodil, 105
Begonia, 26, 30, 36, 48, 53, 54, 60, 66, 80, 124
Begonia, fibrous, 90
Begonia, tuberous, 36, 48, 54, 60, 64-65
Begonia, Wax, 66, 99
Begonia, White Fibrous, 54
Begonia Semperflorens, 47, 67
Begonia Society, American, 64
Bell, Canterbury, 125
Belladonna, 15
Bellamosum, 15
Bellflower, Dalmation. *See* Dalmation Bellflower.
Bellflower, dwarf, 106
Bellflower family, 125
Bells-of-Ireland, 12, 24, 65, 69, 80, 90, 100, 110, 120, 122, 130
Bergenia Crassifolia, 99
Bertini hybrids, 54, 64
Biennial, 131
Big Blue Lily Turf, 65-66
Bird of Paradise, 124, 125
Bittersweet Lily, 128
Black Dragon Lily, 128
Black-eyed Susan, 68
Blanket Flower. *See* Gaillardia.
Blazing Star, 97
Bloom fertilizer, 74, 77, 98, 131
Blossom drop, 85
Blue Cup Flower, 47, 48, 80
Blue Dicks Ipheon, 119
Blue Lily Turf, 102
Blue Lobelia, 77
Blue Lupine, 97
Blue Marguerite. *See* Felicia.
Blue Parrot Tulip, 105
Bone meal, 18, 21, 27, 38, 41, 61, 66, 92, 102, 127, 132
Botanicals, 131
Bradshaw, Mrs., Geum, 77
Breeder Tulips, 104
Broadcasting, 131
Browning of leaf edges, 82
Bubbler, 62
Bud (eye), 113
Bud union, 21, 131
Bulb(s), 2, 4-5, 12, 24, 36, 48, 50, 70, 97-98, 109, 110, 119, 120, 122, 126-128, 130
Bulb covers, 114-115, 131
Bulb pan, 8, 131
Bulbils, 67
Burgundy Lily, 128
Burpee, W. Atlee, Co., 45, 108

Burpeeana Zinnia, 68
Butt, Clara, Tulip, 105
Buttercup, Creeping, 114-115
Butterfly Flower, 41, 93, 96, 110, 120

Cacti, 82
de Caen Anemone, 103
Calendula, 2, 11, 12, 24, 41, 84, 90, 99, 100, 110, 120, 124, 130
California Giant Zinnia, 68, 69
California Poppy, 12, 96-97, 109, 120, 130
California Poppy, Ballerina Yellow, 119
Calla Lily, 12, 14-15, 125
Calonyction, 58, 78
Camellia, 2, 26, 38, 50, 60, 83, 88, 102, 124
Campanula, 35, 36, 48, 58, 70, 125
Campanula Portenschlagiana. *See* Dalmation Bellflower.
Canary Bird Flower, 31
Candle Delphinium, 15
Candytuft, 130
Candytuft, annual, 35, 36, 40, 99, 100, 110, 120
Candytuft, perennial, 11, 12, 23, 24, 30, 36, 54, 58, 72, 79, 80, 88, 106, 114
Cane, 131
Canna, 28-29, 48, 102, 113
Canterbury Bell, 125
Carnation, perennial, 6, 36, 48, 58, 70, 80, 100, 110, 120
Carpet Bugle. *See* Ajuga.
Carpet of Snow, 87, 99, 115
Celosia, 60
Centaurea Cineraria, 41, 57, 79
China Aster, 76
Chinese Delphinium, 15
Chinese Houses, 97
Christmas ideas, 122
Chrysanthemum, 30, 39, 41, 50, 58, 60, 70, 74, 80, 90, 100, 110, 122, 124, 130
Cineraria, 2, 6, 24, 100, 120, 130
Cinnabar Lily, 128
Cinquefoil, 88, 115
Cion, 131
Clara Butt Tulips, 105
Clarkia, 12, 97, 110, 120, 130
Climbing Hybrid Teas, 3-4
Climbing Sweet Pea, 100, 110
Clivia miniata. *See* Kafir Lily.
Cockscomb, 48, 70
Cockscomb, Dwarf, 47
Codling moths, 33
Coleus, 25, 29, 30, 47, 48, 58, 66, 70, 80, 89, 90, 102-103
Coloring cut flowers, 54
Columbine, 12, 48, 120, 130
Columbine, Rocky Mountain, 23
Compost, 2, 18, 21, 26, 27, 28, 42, 43, 51, 56, 61, 64, 66, 82, 92, 94-95, 102, 108, 132
Coral Bells, 12, 24, 36, 48, 58, 69, 70, 76, 93, 110, 120, 130
Coreopsis, 57, 90, 130
Corm, 18, 51, 97, 118, 124, 131
Cormels, 131

Cosmos, 48, 57, 70, 80, 90
Cottage Tulips, 104
Cottonseed meal, 26
Cragford, 105
Crassifloria, Bergenia, 99
Creeping Buttercup, 16, 114-115
Crimson Beauty Lily, 128
Crocus, 110
Crossing, 131
Crown, 4, 131
Crown gall, 83
Cup-and-Saucer Canterbury Bell, 125
Cupid Zinnia, 68
Cut-and-Come Again, 46
Cutting, 131
Cuttings, propagation from, 30
Cuttings, semi-hardwood, 73
Cyclamen, 2, 119, 130
Cyclaminius-type daffodils, 105

Daffodil, 12, 104-108, 114, 120, 130
Daffodil, February Gold, 119
Daffodil, Fortune, 129
Daffodil, Francisca Drake, 129
Daffodil, King Alfred, 105, 109
Daffodil garlic, 117
Daffodil Narcissus. See Daffodil.
Dahlia, 30, 36, 39, 40, 41-42, 58, 60, 70, 74, 90, 113
Daisy, African, 24, 100, 110, 130
Daisy, English, 12, 23, 100, 110, 115, 120, 130
Daisy, Gloriosa, 36, 68, 90
Daisy, Shasta, 24, 35, 36, 39, 54, 80, 83, 100, 120
Daisy, Transvaal, 11, 51, 74
Dalmatian Bellflower, 35, 36, 48, 69, 70, 76-77, 88, 125
Damping-off, 9, 52, 131
Dandelion digger, 17
Darwin Hybrid class tulips, 104
Davids & Royston Bulb Company, 127
Daylily, 36, 48, 49, 53, 56, 83-84, 103, 125
Deciduous, 14, 131
Deep watering, 131
Delphinium, 12, 15-16, 36, 38, 48, 58, 74, 100, 110, 120, 122, 130
Delphinium, Pacific Giants, 15
Descanso Gardens, 2
Detergents, 33
Dianthus, 30, 41, 48, 57, 58, 70, 80
Dormancy, artificial, 104
Dormant, 2, 14, 124, 131
Double Late tulips, 104
Doubles, 85
Drainage, 131
Dried flowers as gifts, 122
Drip line, 132
Drought-tolerant flowers, 88, 92-93, 116
Dusty Miller, 41, 57, 79
Dutch hoe, 17
Dutch Iris, 109, 120, 130
Dwarf Baboon Flower, 124
Dwarf Bellflowers, 106
Dwarf Marigold, 45, 69
Dwarf Pompon Zinnia, 69

Dwarf Sunflower, 46
Earth up, 47, 132
Eckert, William, 66
Edema, 52
Edgebrook Shasta Daisy, 54
Edging plants, 106-107, 122
Edible plants, 34, 37, 44, 45-46, 56, 85
Eisenhower, Gen., Tulips, 105
Elizabeth Arden Tulips, 105
Enchantment Lily, 128
English Daisy, 12, 23, 100, 110, 115, 120, 130
English Primrose, 7, 24, 99, 120, 130
Entomology, Bureau of, California Department of Agriculture, 33
Envy Zinnia, 68
Epiphyte, 67
Erosion, 82, 86, 132. See Ground cover.
Escape, 53
Evergreen Candytuft, 88
Evergreen foliage, 7, 14, 29, 65, 76, 77, 88, 117
Extension rod, 62-63
Eye (bud), 113, 132

Fairy Primrose, 7, 99, 100, 110, 120
Fairy Star, 97, 99
Fall soil conditioning, 92
Fallow, 106
Feather Cockscomb, 71, 77, 79
Felicia, 2, 31, 47, 79, 80
Fern, 26, 53, 60, 64, 67-68, 124
Ferry-Morse, 108
Fertilizing, 26-27, 38, 64, 65, 74, 77, 83, 84, 98, 124, 127, 131
Fire Opal Geum, 77
First Lady Marigold, 45, 78
Fish fertilizer, 2, 6, 14, 27, 28, 29, 38, 40, 42, 51, 56, 60, 64, 67, 74, 75, 82, 98, 107, 117, 125
Flats, 8
Florence Nightingale Gladiola, 55
Floribundas, 3, 61
Floriferous, 126, 132
Flossflower. See Ageratum.
Flowers, dried, 122
Fogger nozzle, 62, 65
Foliar feeding, 132
Forget-me-not, 12, 24, 35, 48, 58, 100, 110, 120, 130
Fortune Daffodil, 129
Fourth of July "beauty spot," 35
Foxglove, 12, 24, 84, 100, 110, 120, 130
Francisca Drake Daffodil, 129
Freesia, 91, 97, 110, 120, 130
Freeway Daisy. See African Daisy, Trailing.
French Marigold, 45
French Marigold, Dwarf, 89
Friable, 132
Frost, 2, 125
Fuchsia 26, 28, 30, 36, 42-43, 48, 53, 60, 66, 67, 74, 124
Fungus, Watermold, 35
Fungus diseases, 27, 53, 73, 76, 107, 112

Gaillardia, 1, 6, 36, 48, 58, 70, 79, 80, 90, 110, 120, 130
Galaxy (bush-type) Sweet Pea, 108
Gall, crown, 83
Garden Party Tulip (Triumph class), 104
Garden planning, 2, 72
Garland delphinium, 15
Garlic, 22, 117
Garlic, Daffodil, 117
Garlic, Golden, 117
Gazania, 36, 48, 58, 70, 80, 86-87
Geranium, 30, 40, 41, 43-44, 58, 70, 80
Geranium Ivy, 88
Geranium and Pearlgonium Show, Los Angeles, 43
Geranium Society, International, Southwest Branch, 43
Geranium tea, 44
Gerbera, 11, 51, 74
Gestatio, 72
Geum, 36, 48, 77, 79
Giant Allium, 33, 116-117
Giant Imperial Stock(s), 99
Giant Ruffled Snapdragon, 98
Gift ideas (Christmas), 122
Gilia, 97, 99
Gladiola(s), 12, 17, 18-19, 36, 48, 51, 55, 58, 70, 113-114
Globe Candytuft, 40, 130
Gloriosa Daisy, 36, 48, 68, 70, 80, 90
Gloriosa lilies, 125
Gloxinoides. See Penstemon.
Godetia, 12, 23, 100, 110, 120, 130
Golden Fleece, 77
Golden garlic, 117
Golden Splendor Lily, 128
de Graaff, Jan, 127-128
Grandifloras, 3
Green Magic Lily, 128
Greigii class tulips, 104
Ground covers, 86-88, 106, 114-115, 127, 132

Halcro Tulips, 105
Harlequin Flower. See Sparaxis.
Helianthus Giganteus. See Sunflower.
Heliotrope, 11, 30
Hemerocallis. See Daylily.
Herniaria, 87, 115
Herbst, Margaret, Tulip, 105
Hollyhock, 12, 13, 19-20, 36, 41, 48, 100, 110, 120, 130
Holmes, Thomas R., 127
Hose-in-hose, 4, 125, 132
Hoses, 123
Hottentot Fig, 88
Humus, 95, 132
Hunnemannia, 47
Hyacinth, 4-5, 110
Hybrid Teas, 3
Hybrids, 126, 132

Iberis sempervirens. See Candytuft, perennial.
Iceland Poppy, 24, 81, 84, 85, 100, 110, 120, 122, 130
Impatiens, 74, 80

Imperial Crimson Lily, 128
Imperial Gold Lily, 128
Imperial Silver Lily, 128
Indian Blanket. See Gaillardia.
Insecticide, 32-33, 131
Insecticide, systemic, 28, 32
Insects and pests, 14, 22, 28, 29, 31-33, 42, 43, 44, 54, 74, 103, 117
Ipheon, Blue Dicks, 119
Iris, Bearded, 60-61, 74, 93, 103, 120, 124
Iris, Dutch, 109, 120, 130
Irish Eyes. See Gloriosa Daisy.
Irrigation, 21, 68
Ivy Geranium, 88

Jamboree Lily, 128
Japanese Iris, blue, 77
Japanese Spurge, 88
Jewel of Spring Tulips, 105
Joan Evans Lily, 128
Jonquil. See Daffodil.

Kafir Lily, 117, 119, 120
King Alfred Daffodil, 105, 109
Knee-Hi Sweet Pea, Bush, 108
Kochia, 58, 70, 78
Kurume, 4

Lady bug, 33
Lady Stratheden Geum, 77
Lady Washington Geranium, 43
Lantana, Trailing, 88
Larkspur, 15, 24, 70, 90, 100, 110, 120. See also Delphinium.
Lateral, 132
Leaching, 82, 132
Leaf hoppers, 32, 43
Leaf mold, 18, 42-43, 64, 92, 108
Leaf spot, bacterial, 43
Leaf worms, 43
Leather fern, 67
Lee, Charles, v
Lifting, 55
Lilium, 125
Lily, 12, 24, 103, 110, 120, 121, 125-128
Lily, Kafir, 117, 119, 120
Lily, true, 125
Lily Flowered Tulips, 104
Lily-of-the-Nile. See Agapanthus.
Lily-of-the-Valley, 12, 20, 130
Linaria, 106, 120
Linum, 109, 120
Living mulch, 88, 114-115, 127
Loam, 132
Lobelia, 11, 24, 77, 110, 120
Luminarias, 122-123
Lupine, Blue, 96-97

Madagascar Periwinkle. See Vinca Rosea.
Madonna Lily, 4
Magic Pink Lily, 128
Maidenhair Fern, 66-67
Maier, C. E., 82
Majestic Shasta Daisy, 54
Manure, 27-28, 38, 41, 93, 95, 127, 132
Mariette Tulips, 105, 119
Marigold, 35, 36, 39, 44-45, 58, 69, 70, 78, 80, 90

Margaret Herbst Tulip, 105
Marguerite, 2, 31, 48, 58, 70, 79, 80
Martha Washington, 43
Matilija Poppy, 11
Maureen Tulip, 105
May Wonder Tulip, 105
Maytime Tulip, 105
Mealybugs, 29, 32, 117
Mendel Tulips, 104
Mesembryanthemum, 88
Mexican Fire Bush, 58, 70, 78
Mid-Century Hybrid Lilies, 128
Mignonette, 11, 24, 70, 100, 110, 120
Mildew, 53, 68
Miniature flower beds, 89
Misting, 65
Mites, spider, 32-33
Mockingbird Flowers, 64
Monarch de Caen Anemone, 119
Moonflower, 58, 78
Morning Glory, 78
Morocco Toadflax, 106
Moss, sphagnum, 67
Mossholder Gold Cup Hybrids, 4
Mother Fischer Gladiola, 55
Mother Spleenwort Fern, 67
Mother-of-Thyme, 87-88
Moths, codling, 33
Mount Tacoma Tulips, 105
Mulch, 18, 107, 132
Mulch, living, 88, 114-115, 127
Mulching, 6, 14, 18, 42, 56, 82, 107
Multiflora Nana, 6

Naked Lady. See Amaryllis.
Narcissus, 105
Nasturtium, 31, 34, 41, 48, 58, 69, 70, 74-75, 80
Nasturtium, Dwarf, 89
Naturalize, 97, 104, 117, 132
Nematodes, 44
Nemesia, 23, 41
Nemophila, 100
Nicotiana, 80, 90, 100, 110
Nierembergia, 47, 48, 80
Night-blooming Moonflower, 78
Nitrogen, 2, 27, 35, 40, 42, 51, 95, 124. See also Fertilizers.
North American Lily Society, 125
Nugget Marigold, 45, 78
Nymph, 28, 132. See also Thrips.

Onion, 116-117
Oregon Bulb Farms, 127-128
Oriental dried Daylilies (edible), 56
Oriental Hybrid Mix Lilies, 128
Oriental Poppy, 11
Ornithogalum, 129
Osteospermum. See African Daisy, Trailing.
Other plantables, 12, 24, 36, 48, 58, 70, 80, 90, 100, 110, 120, 130
Overhead watering, 53
Overwatering, 52, 53

Painted Tongue, 12, 24, 41, 69, 80, 90, 100, 110, 120
Pansy, 2, 12, 24, 35, 40, 75, 90,

100, 101, 106-107, 109, 120, 124, 130
Paper White, 105
Paris Daisy. See Marguerite.
Parrot Tulip, 104
Parsley, 33
Patient Lucy, 74, 80
Payne Foundation, Theodore, 96-97
Pearl, Tuberose, 55
Peat moss, 4, 18, 28, 43, 51, 56, 92, 108, 113
Peeping Tom, 105-106
Pelargonium. See Geranium.
Peltate, 31
Penstemon, 6-7, 24, 47, 48, 100, 110, 120, 130
Perennial Candytuft. See Candytuft, perennial.
Perennial, 132
Perennials, 7, 60, 73, 82-83, 98
Periwinkle, 88
Pests. See Insects and Pests.
Petal blight, 2
Peter Pan Zinnia, 68-69
Petunia, 2, 11, 24, 34-35, 41, 47, 48, 58, 70, 80, 100, 110, 120, 130
Phacelia, large-flowered, 97
Phlox, annual, 24, 36, 41, 48, 55, 80, 90, 100, 110, 120
Phosphorus, 27
Pickled Nasturtium, 34
Picotee, 132
Picotees, 64
Pinching back, 41, 93, 132
Pincushion Flower (Scabiosa), 36, 77, 100, 110
Pink Glory Lily, 128
Pink Perfection Lily, 128
Pips, 20
Pirate Lily, 128
Plant divisions, 36, 48, 58
Plant food, 83
Plantain extractor, 17
Planting mix, 67, 83, 126, 132. See also Potting mix.
Plumed Knight, 71, 77, 79
Plunging, 114, 132
Pods, seed, 118
Poet's narcissus, 106
Poinsettias, 39, 51
Pony packs, 8
Poor Man's Azalea, 43
Poor Man's Orchid. See Butterfly Flower.
Poppy, California, 12, 41, 96-97, 109, 119, 120, 130
Poppy, Iceland, 24, 81, 84-85, 100, 110, 120, 130
Poppy, Matilija, 11
Poppy, Oriental, 11
Poppy, Shirley, 117-118, 119
Poppy-flowered Anemone, 129
Portulaca, 36, 48, 58, 70, 80, 86-87
Pot Marigold. See Calendula.
Pot-bound, 43
Potentilla Cinerea, 88, 115
Potentilla Verna, 115
Pot-in-pot propagation, 30, 73
Potting mix, 9, 30, 83, 132. See also Planting mix.

Pricking out, 132
Primrose, 23, 26, 61, 122, 124
Primrose, English, 7, 24, 99, 120, 130
Primrose, Fairy, 99, 100, 110, 120
Princess Juliana Geum, 77
Progression, 132
Prosperity Lily, 128
Prostrate spurge, 16
Pups, 67
Pyrethrum, 33, 43

Queen of Sheba Tulip, 105

Rabbit's Paw Fern, 67
Raffia, 75
Rainbow Hybrid Lilies, 128
Rainbow Mixture, 96
Raised bed, 126-127
Ramets, 83
Ranunculus, 108, 120, 129, 130
Red Flare Lily, 128
Regal Geranium, 43
Regale Lily, 128
Resurgence, 32
Rhizomes, 15, 28, 60, 61, 132
Rogelli Shasta Daisy, 54
Root aphis, 76
Root feeder, 63
Root rot, 52, 107
Root-bound, 43
Rosarian, 132
Roses, 3-4, 14, 20-22, 28, 33, 38, 51-52, 61, 62, 84, 93, 117
Rosea, 48
Rose-soaker, 62
Rot, 73, 113
Rotation, 132
Rotenone (botanical), 33, 43
Royal Carpet, 87
Rubro cyanea, 124
Rupturewort, 87, 115
Rust, 98
Rutherfordiana, 4

St. Brigid Anemone, 103
Salt buildup, 82
Salvia, 36, 48, 57, 70, 80
Sand, 56, 66, 113
Sawdust, 18, 113
Saxatile, Alyssum. See Alyssum Saxatile.
Scabiosa, 36, 48, 57, 100, 110, 120
Scarlet Flax, 109, 120
Scheepers, Mrs. John T., Tulip, 105
Schizanthus. See Butterfly Flower.
Scilla, 129
Scion, 131
Shuffle hoe, 17
Sea Pink, 88
Seeds, 2, 8-10, 12, 14, 24, 35, 36, 47, 48, 57, 58, 69, 70, 79, 80, 89, 90, 99, 100, 109, 110, 119, 120, 129, 130
Seed leaves, 132
Seed pods, removing, 56, 118
Seedlings, 9-10, 50, 52, 132
Seedling nozzle, 62
Semi-hardwood cuttings, 72-73
Setting buds, 27

Shasta Daisy, 24, 35, 36, 39, 54, 80, 83, 100, 120
Shirley Poppy, 117-118, 119
Siberian delphinium, 15
Siberian Squill, 129
Single Late Tulips, 104
Singles, 85
Sitfast, 16, 114-115
Slugs. See Snails.
Snails, 14, 32, 44, 54, 74, 103
Snapdragon, 12, 24, 41, 98, 99, 110, 120, 130
Snapdragon, Giant Ruffled, 98
Snowbank, 47, 67
Soaker-sprinkler, 63, 123
Softwood cuttings, propagation from, 30
Softwood plants, 30
Soil, 27, 38, 43, 60, 66, 82, 92, 94, 95
Soleil d'Or, 105
Southern Indica, 4
Sowing, 131
Sparaxis, 110, 111, 118, 120, 129, 130
Sphagnum moss, 67
Spider mites, 32-33, 42
Sponge rock, 67
Sprays, 32-33
Spring bulbs, 102
Staghorn Fern, 67
Staking, 39, 102
Star, Fairy, 99
Star of Bethlehem, 129
State Fair Zinnia, 68
Steer manure. See Manure.
Stem bulblets, 103
Suckers, 51-52
Stem mold, 65
Stem rot, 44
Stepping stones, 87
Stock, 2, 12, 24, 85, 100, 109, 110, 120, 124, 130
Stock, Giant Imperial, 99
Stock, Virginia, 100, 110, 120, 130
Strawflower, 89, 120, 122
Strelitzia, 124-125
Strelitzia reginae, 125
Succulents, 82
Sucker, 132
Sulfur, 113
Sulphurea, 124
Sunburn, plant, 53
Sunflower, 37, 39, 41, 45-46, 47, 58, 70, 80
Sunkist Tulip, 105
Superphosphate, 92
Sweeper nozzle, 53
Sweet Alyssum, 11, 12, 36, 48, 58, 60, 70, 80, 86-87, 99, 100, 106, 110, 115, 116, 130
Sweet Pea, 22, 41, 130
Sweet Pea, Bush, 24, 100, 108, 120
Sweet Pea, Climbing, 100, 110
Sweet Violet, 85-87
Sweet William, 110
Sword Fern, 66
Systemic insecticide, 28, 32

Tasmanian Tree Fern, 67
Tea, Violet, 85

Terminal, 132
Texas Gold Tulip, 105
Texas Flame Tulip, 105
Theodore Payne Foundation, 96
Thinning, 132
Thrips, 28, 32-33
Thumbelina Shasta Daisy, 54
Thumbelina Zinnia, 69
Tidytip, 109
Tilth, 18, 132
Tom Thumb Zinnias, 89
Tools, 122-123
Top dressing, 132
Top soil, 127
Trailing Lantana, 88
Transplanting seedlings, 10
Transvaal Daisy, 51
Tree ferns, Australian and Tasmanian, 67
Tree roses, 4
Trees, deciduous, 117
Triumph Tulip, 104
Triumphator, White, 119
Tuberose, 48, 55
Tuberous Begonia. See Begonia, tuberous.
Tubers, 58
Tulip, 4-6, 103-105, 110, 114
Tulip, Mariette, 119

Union, bud, 21, 131
Unwins, 42

Vacationing plants, 114
Verbena, Garden, 7, 24, 30, 35, 36, 41, 48, 58, 70, 80, 100, 110, 120
Vinca, 30, 48
Vinca Minor, 88
Vinca Rosea, 36, 48, 55, 60, 80
Viola, 90, 99, 106-107, 109, 110, 120, 130
Violet Queen, 11
Violet, Sweet, 85-87
Violet tea, 85
Virginia Stock, 100, 110, 115, 120, 130
Vonk, Alice, 45

Wand Flower, 111, 118
Watering, 52-53, 68, 82, 92, 131
Watering tools, 53, 62-63
Watermold fungus, 36
Wax Begonia, 66, 99
Wedgwood, 109, 120, 130
Weeding, 14, 16-17
White City Tulip, 105
White Champion, Spec., Lily, 128
White flies, 32, 43
White gardens, 54-55
White Marigold, 45
White Triumphator, 119
Wild flowers, 24, 96, 120, 130
William, Sweet, 110
Wilt, 107
Wind, 102, 112

Yellows, 76

Zenith Zinnia, 68
Zinnia, 38, 41, 58, 59, 60, 68, 69, 79, 80, 90
Zonals, 43